"Even our best ideas can, over time, become ruts that stifle creativity. In *The Integrative Mindset*, two outstanding clinicians, supervisors, and theoreticians jump out of the integration rut and give us much to ponder. Their notion of 'integrative moments' bends our current paradigms, offers fresh perspectives, and calls us to stand in wonder at what often happens in the clinical office."

Mark R. McMinn, professor emeritus at George Fox University, and coauthor with Megan Anna Neff, of *Embodying Integration*

"If you want to enrich your clinical integration capacities, then read this book! Brad D. Strawn and Earl D. Bland guide you through ways to embody a 'thick' integrative presence with your clients that will rekindle the wonder of joining God in God's work in your clients' lives."

Virginia T. Holeman, emeritus professor of counseling at Asbury Theological Seminary and author of *Theology for Better Counseling*

"*The Integrative Mindset* is a paradigm-shifting contribution to the field and an essential guide for Christian clinicians seeking to enhance their practice with wisdom, integrity, and faith. With intellectual depth and practical insight, Brad D. Strawn and Earl D. Bland help clinicians navigate the intersections of faith, ethics, and tradition in a way that is both responsive and flexible. A must-read for clinicians, supervisors, professors, and students committed to thoughtful and ethical integrative clinical practice."

William B. Whitney, associate professor of psychology at Azusa Pacific University

THE INTEGRATIVE MINDSET

PATHWAYS TO PRACTICING AS A CHRISTIAN CLINICIAN

Brad D. Strawn & Earl D. Bland

An imprint of InterVarsity Press
Downers Grove, Illinois

InterVarsity Press
P.O. Box 1400 | Downers Grove, IL 60515-1426
ivpress.com | email@ivpress.com

©2025 by Brad D. Strawn and Earl D. Bland

All rights reserved. No part of this book may be reproduced in any form without written permission from InterVarsity Press.

InterVarsity Press® is the publishing division of InterVarsity Christian Fellowship/USA®. For more information, visit intervarsity.org.

All Scripture quotations, unless otherwise indicated, are taken from The Holy Bible, New International Version®, NIV®. Copyright © 1973, 1978, 1984, 2011 by Biblica, Inc.™ Used by permission of Zondervan. All rights reserved worldwide. www.zondervan.com. The "NIV" and "New International Version" are trademarks registered in the United States Patent and Trademark Office by Biblica, Inc.™

While any stories in this book are true, some names and identifying information may have been changed to protect the privacy of individuals.

"This Is Just to Say," by William Carlos Williams, is from *The Collected Poems*, Volume I, 1909-1939, copyright ©1938 by New Directions Publishing Corp. Reprinted by permission of New Directions Publishing Corp.

"A Poem That Came Easily," by Yun Dong-ju, is reprinted with permission from Asian Humanities Press, a division of Jain Publishing Company, www.jainpub.com.

The publisher cannot verify the accuracy or functionality of website URLs used in this book beyond the date of publication.

Cover design: Faceout Studio, Jeff Miller
Interior design: Daniel van Loon
Images: © GeorgePeters / DigitalVision Vectors via Getty Images

ISBN 978-1-5140-0220-9 (print) | ISBN 978-1-5140-0221-6 (digital)

Printed in the United States of America ∞

Library of Congress Cataloging-in-Publication Data
A catalog record for this book is available from the Library of Congress.

| 31 | 30 | 29 | 28 | 27 | 26 | 25 | | 13 | 12 | 11 | 10 | 9 | 8 | 7 | 6 | 5 | 4 | 3 | 2 | 1 |

We'd like to acknowledge and dedicate this book to all our mentors, students, colleagues, and clients.

You have taught us, put up with us teaching these ideas through the years, and wrestled with us in clinical spaces. Your influence has formed us in profound ways, and we pray it has been mutual.

CONTENTS

(A Kind of) Introduction	1
1 Emergence Matters *Illuminating the Integrative Moment*	5
2 Hermeneutics Matter *Setting the Table*	32
3 Tradition Matters *The Hermeneutics of Theological Location*	64
4 Ethics Matter *The Hermeneutics of Ultimacy*	89
5 Self-Development Matters *The Hermeneutics of Formation*	110
6 Resilience Matters *The Hermeneutics of Nourishing Emergence*	135
(A Kind of) Conclusion	165
References	169
Name Index	179
Subject Index	181

(A KIND OF) INTRODUCTION

Please do not skip this introduction.

This is not your typical book introduction. In this introduction we share with you *why* we dared to write this book. In so doing, we invite you into a conversation, a dialogue—we let you into our clinical integrative minds in hopes that they will affect yours.

If you've read this far, the dialogue has already begun! Reading a book is like having a conversation, even if mostly one sided. We can't know what you are thinking or feeling, but we trust that you will be, and that is our desire. Our subjective experience affects yours, and so we believe that thinking, feeling, pondering, destabilizing, and confirming are all happening even if we don't get to hear your side. This book is born out of hundreds of conversations between the two of us, with our students, and even in the clinical setting. We trust that your dialogue with us will include (from your side) interactions with beliefs you have held up to this point, with people who have been important in your training and now live in your memory, and maybe even with others who are also reading the book. We provide some reflective questions toward the ends of the chapters to facilitate this conversation.

Ultimately, we hope you will feel invited into our clinical integrative minds. We are not trying to persuade you that our approach to practicing *as* Christian clinicians (e.g., clinical integrative practice), is the best; we aren't looking for disciples. We are not offering a Christian therapy but a way to think about therapy that takes religious faith seriously. For us, that faith is Christianity, which animates everything we do as clinicians. What we are attempting is to let you in on how we, two integrative clinicians who have each been practicing for over thirty years (over sixty years total!), think about our work. We believe that the process of practicing in clinically integrative ways is too highly idiosyncratic to each therapist/counselor and therapy dyad for a one-size-fits-all approach. Therefore, it is quite difficult to say what makes a therapy Christian. We are not playing the game of who is in and who is out.

However, practicing clinical integration does not preclude learning from others. This is why it is a dialogue. In this book we attempt to share with you what we have been thinking, feeling, and embodying these past sixty-odd years, and we invite you to play with it, destroy it, rearrange it, take it apart, and put it back together again—just make it your own. Keep what's helpful. Throw out what doesn't fit. Life and therapy are too deeply influenced by one's particular social location to do otherwise.

As we were conceiving this book, we asked each other, "How did we learn to engage in clinical integrative practice?" While we both benefited greatly from theories and models, it was the dialogues we had with peers, professors, and especially supervisors that we found most helpful. In these dialogues we experienced ways of thinking integratively. We are thankful that we (mostly) never had supervisors force their approach on us or make us into therapeutic ventriloquist dummies. Instead, supervisors (the ones who had the greatest and lasting impact) modeled ways of working, ways of conceptualizing and feeling, offered possibilities; they let us into their clinical integrative minds. They showed rather than told us why integration matters. These were certainly eye-opening and informative conversations, but what they mostly did was awaken our imaginations.

Dialogue is not easy. Often in life, when we become anxious, we resort to debate, where there are winners and losers. But dialogue is a vulnerable space in which both participants hold their experiences lightly, and subsequently both participants might be changed. So, beware! If you read this book, you might be changed. You might be challenged, and you might be exposed to ideas and experiences that cause you to feel—even feel deeply. How will you respond if something surprises you, doesn't fit for you, or even rubs you the wrong way? Will you throw the whole thing out, or will you risk staying in dialogue? Will you search for resonance and anything helpful that you might take back to your situation, setting, and social location and make your own? Will you be tempted to dismiss it all, saying something like, "That's not Christian"? We have found that we have learned much from those with whom we disagree, if we can manage our anxiety and hold the dialogical tension.

We believe that it's in the intersubjective space of a two-person dialogue that imagination emerges and change occurs. In a sense this is not unlike the work of therapy. So, we invite you to imagine that you are having coffee (or your beverage of choice) with a couple of supervisors, talking about their experiences, viewpoints, and perspectives on clinical integrative practice. Again, these conversations are not prescriptions or mandates. This is not a book of clinical integrative practice indoctrination, and we don't believe we are espousing The Christian Perspective or a form of Christian therapy. We trust the God of Christian faith to be at work in the clinical encounter. Whether the work is *Christian* or *spiritual* or something else is entirely up to God. We hope you will find it inviting and even humble in its approach: open, welcoming, and hospitable to edits and nuance. We have consistently said over our years of teaching that we have no desire to turn students into ourselves or even some kind of prototype of the clinical integrative practitioner. We want to help students find their own particular way or voice to be a clinical integrative practitioner, leaning into all their experiences and God-given talents.

We said this wasn't your typical introduction, but let us amend that ever so slightly and offer an overview of the book. In chapter one we will introduce you to our understanding of how integrative moments emerge in therapy through the process of dynamic systems theory. This perspective points toward the importance of holding a particular mindset in therapy that allows the complexity of the therapist-client dyad to potentially facilitate integrative moments. This integrative mindset is marked by five domains: hermeneutics, tradition, ethics, self-development, and resilience. In chapter two we explore the centrality of hermeneutics as an interpretive discipline that is central to therapeutic understanding and the bedrock of the other domains. Chapter three explores the domain of tradition, which is a deeper look at where our hermeneutics come from especially as they relate to religious or spiritual traditions. Chapter four is about the hermeneutical and tradition-based ethics embedded in our professions, personal lives, theories, and even communities. Our ethical commitments, which include images of *how* one *should* live and images of the good life, are often implicit and can create conflicts between therapist and client, therapist and their theory, and other permutations. In chapter five we bring this all together to assist you to explicitly mine the first three domains as a function of your particularity. Finally, in chapter six, we offer some ways to help the integrative clinician stay not only resilient in their career over the years but attuned to what God is up to in the therapy.

So, can we chat?

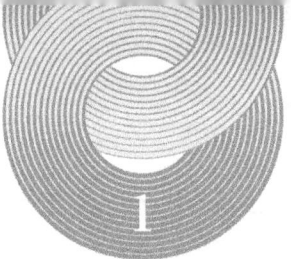

EMERGENCE MATTERS
ILLUMINATING THE INTEGRATIVE MOMENT

It's the first session with a brand-new client. Paperwork has been filled out, introductions have been made, you and the client have both sat down on comfortable furniture, and now you've invited the client to explain what has brought them to see you today. But instead of answering your question, they turn and ask, "You're religious, right?"

What do you say? Why is the client asking this? What *exactly* are they asking? Is this a trap, a defense, an attack, a plea for attachment and solidarity, or something else entirely? How do you incorporate this into therapeutic work? Is talking about religion even okay in therapy? What if the client wants to say more about their faith or is interested in yours? What if they want to talk about what their faith has to do with their psychological issues? Is this a moment of integration of psychology and theology, and if so, what do you do?

Over the years we have had the privilege of conducting and supervising therapy with countless clients who professed religious faith. So, over the years we have heard lots of stories. We have worked with deeply religious clients who said they were afraid to come to therapy because they were told by their Christian friends and pastors that psychology was dangerous and should be avoided.

We've heard these same believers say that instead of coming to counseling they were told that they should have more faith and pray harder. Yet somehow, when all their religious resources disappointed them, they found their way to our offices. On the other end of the spectrum, we have had religious clients come to us saying that if we even mentioned God or the Bible, they would find another therapist. We've even had nonreligious clients say that they had come to see us because even though they were not religious, they thought that maybe there was something spiritual in the world that they might benefit from thinking more about.

We have also had the honor of training students of faith to become psychologists or counselors who were authentically intent in their desire to bring together religion/spirituality with their psychological knowledge. From these students we have also heard stories. Students have told us that they love psychology and love their faith, but they just can't get their mind around how to put these two into meaningful conversation, especially in practical ways they can apply in their clinical work. We have had students wonder whether they are truly integrating their faith into their practice if they are not talking about God or Scripture or engaging in some practice of faith. We have had students (and peers) who were so afraid of integrating faith poorly that they consciously (and unconsciously) avoided the subject altogether, even when the client practically brought it up. We've had students who prayed with a client as soon as the client asked for it and others who adamantly refused, saying, "I'm a psychologist, not a pastor." We've even had students who, while not afraid to ask clients about their personal sex life, finances, or their culture, were terrified to bring up the issue of religion or spirituality, saying, "It's just so personal."

In general, we find that the idea of integration is attractive and desired by our students and colleagues, but the actual embodiment of an integrative clinical posture has been somewhat illusive. We especially find this with our students from various non-White cultures, who often remark that the writing, research, and theorizing around the integration of psychology and theology is primarily White, patriarchal, and of a Reformed theological persuasion.

So, while *integration*, a term we will define below, has been around for at least fifty years, there is still much confusion about what it is, how to define it, and, for the focus of this book, how to engage it in clinical practice. Our desire is to make the clinical experience of integration more accessible and applicable to everyday work with clients. We specifically want to address the gap so many Christian therapists and counselors encounter when they attempt to bridge the theory or idea of integration and the real-world clinical relationships.

We begin by drawing a parallel with a phrase that our good friend and early integrator John Carter was fond of saying. John would often say that Christians were interested in "thinking Christian thoughts," but they should be more concerned with "thinking Christianly." We believe too that many Christian therapists are interested in "integrative thoughts" (e.g., models, formulas, manuals), but we want to challenge integrators to "think integratively." Semantically, an adverb always modifies another word and usually answers a question such as "How?" If one is thinking Christianly, *Christianly* is modifying the verb *thinking*, and therefore we can expect that there is some *process* to how one is thinking. In *thinking integratively*, *integratively* modifies *thinking* and also suggests a process or a how. Importantly, when we say *thinking* in this context, we are not referring to an abstract intellectual process, although clearly that is an element of what we are considering. Rather, because all thinking is embodied, we recognize that thinking is a deeply affective experience. Consequently, integrative practice involves the total you—thoughts, feelings, emotional states, and bodily sensations. This book is our attempt to offer a process of *how* to think integratively, or perhaps how to *be* integrative, and why it matters. This process will include five domains (the *matters* that make integration matter): hermeneutics, tradition, ethics, self-development, and resilience. But first let us return to integration itself.

A BRIEF HISTORY OF INTEGRATION TOLD IN FIVE WAVES

While there is an entire literature on interdisciplinary work, some of which we will touch on in later chapters, our focus is on the integration of psychology and theology. In 1953 psychologist Fritz Kunkel first used the term *integration* to describe interdisciplinary activity between psychology and theology. While Kunkel was a major pioneer in the fledgling integration movement, the pastoral psychology movement grabbed hold of the phrase and begin to popularize it (Vande Kemp, 1996). Over time, integration has come to mean many things.

Since the fifties the term *integration* has been used in diverse ways, including (but not limited to) the integration of psychology and Christianity, psychology and religion, psychology and theology (faith and practice, belief and life), psychology and Christian faith, psychology and spirituality, and even psychotherapy and spirituality (Strawn, 2016).

For much of its history, the project to find a satisfactory outcome to the meeting of modern psychology and Christianity has been consumed with developing models of engagement that provide a scaffold or framework for the actual work of integration. This endeavor has produced a remarkable number of diverse and thought-provoking books and journal articles, so much so that some have labeled integration a distinct field of study within the field of clinical psychology (Vande Kemp, 1996). At the risk of gross oversimplification, perhaps we can think broadly of five waves of discourse that characterize this historical conversation—the apologetic wave, the modeling wave, the applied/empirical validation wave, the spiritual formation wave, and the clinical integrative wave (Bland & Strawn, 2024; Strawn, et al., 2018).

Wave one: Apologetic. In the early days of integration, specifically in Christian evangelical and mainline circles, the conversations generally consisted of justifications regarding why such a dialogue might be useful and even compatible with Christian faith. Because the discipline of psychology largely developed within non-Christian institutions and universities, more conservative and evangelical expressions of Christianity were wary of the development of healing methods that addressed people's thoughts, motivations, and behavior—their *hearts*, if you will—absent a clear reference to the beliefs and practices of Christianity. Many were suspicious of and even hostile to the supposed godlessness of psychoanalysis, behaviorism, or existential/humanistic theories. In response to the gap, early work conducted by faculty at Fuller School of Psychology and Rosemead School of Psychology argued persuasively that psychology and Christian faith didn't have to be strange bedfellows but could be allies in both understanding human nature and partnering in the healing and restoration of human difficulties. Although the apologetic wave was largely aimed at Christians, both lay and academic, there were some justifications of religion and spirituality to the secular world of psychological science as well.

Wave two: Modeling. While wave one was largely successful in the broadly Christian world, by the mid- to late 1980s and into the mid-1990s, this discussion expanded beyond defending a conversation between psychology and Christianity to one of providing various models of *how* this might be accomplished. Early thinkers such as Paul Clement, Newt Malony, and Richard Gorsuch (Malony & Vande Kemp, 1995), as well as John Carter and Bruce Narramore (1979), among others, developed models of integration. While these were all helpful, they were primarily models with a *view from a distance* in that they were conceptual models rather than imminently and immediately practical models that demonstrated process and methodology. They were *what* models rather than *how* (i.e., process) models. The models increased in complexity as people such as Stan Jones (1986), David Entwistle (2021), Harold Faw (1998), and others expanded the modeling wave, which possibly reached its peak with the publication of *Psychology and Christianity: Four Views* (Johnson & Jones, 2000), later revised to five views (Johnson, 2010). In an interesting, somewhat dis-integrating twist, these authors relegated integration to a viewpoint (i.e., the "integrates view") while offering other viewpoints (i.e., parallels view, Christian psychology view, transformational view, biblical counseling view) on the intersection of psychology and Christianity. In differentiating their models, contributing authors argued for their distinct viewpoints.

Today it is safe to say that there is no unifying model of the integration of psychology and Christian theology. This may again be due to the various domains at work when one is integrating. In a recent work, Malcolm Jeeves and Thomas Ludwig (2018) advocate dropping the term *integration*, suggesting that it is a problematic attempt to make the two disciplines of psychological science and Christian faith say the same thing—what they call *concordism*. Another recent work suggests that integration must be domain specific (Hathaway & Yarhouse, 2021), suggesting that integration looks and acts differently depending on the domain in which one is operating (e.g., theoretical, applied, role). While some may have become leery of the term *integration*, preferring to reinvent new terminology altogether, we still believe it is a useful word and will discuss our particular meaning below.

Wave three: Applied/empirical. While the project to integrate Christianity and psychology is relatively young, the discipline of the *psychology of religion* has been around for some time.[1] One only needs to think of William James's (1994) *The Varieties of Religious Experience*, first presented as the Gifford Lectures in 1901 and 1902. More recently, this third wave has produced an enormous body of research on religious coping, virtue formation (e.g., humility, patience, gratitude), and human development (Balswick et al., 2016), to name just a few areas. In the psychology of religion, the empirical methodology of psychology is used to study religious phenomena or constructs. For example, one might study the efficacy of prayer or religious concepts such as humility or generosity as contributors to the overall mental health of individuals. Conversely, research also shows how some expressions of religiosity may correlate with prejudice, something we would probably deem as largely harmful to human psychological and social health. More recently, we have seen this area of empirical investigation speak more specifically to how one can promote or use religious and spiritual practices to achieve specific mental health outcomes that are congruent with Christian ethics and virtues within the clinical setting (Knabb et al., 2020; Worthington et al., 2013).

While this kind of basic research is often fascinating and formative for future work in the field, too often it strips religious phenomena from the theological contexts that give them meaning and

---

[1] We use the term *integrate* here specifically referring to the dialogue between psychology and Christianity, while also acknowledging that the practice of interdisciplinary integration has a long intellectual history and that our current conversation is a dimension of this tradition.

purpose. The inherent risk in this reductive tilt is the possibility of rendering research findings as thin descriptions of historically, culturally, and theologically rich concepts that only achieve full animation within the embodied communal practices from which they emerge. So, the psychology of religion and the empirical wave, as an integration endeavor, must carefully situate the constructs of study within their theological particularities for true and meaningful findings to emerge. Alvin Dueck and Kevin Reimer (2009) specifically warn against the implicit dangers of professional psychology co-opting indigenous religio-cultural practices into the rubrics of Western psychology, which then proport to *legitimize* them through the colonializing power structures of scientific or empirical research.

Wave four: Spiritual integrative. In our earlier work (Strawn et al. 2018), we had identified four waves of integration (apologetic, modeling, applied/empirical, and clinical), but now we acknowledge an additional wave (and placed it as our new fourth wave)—what we have come to call the spiritual integrative wave (Bland & Strawn, 2024). We will describe the fifth wave later, but for now, the fourth wave is characterized by the application of research findings and clinical theory to the process of spiritual formation within persons. While spiritual formation has a long history within various church traditions, it has only been recently that this historically religious practice has engaged the professional world of psychology. This has led to a robust and fruitful conversation, which at times has created some blurring of lines but mostly has provided the opportunity for new ways of discussing the intersection between psychology and the church. William James's *Varieties of Religious Experience* may be one of the earliest examples. Other areas of research include growth in moral and/or spiritual maturity (Benner, 2011; Carpenter, 2020; Collicutt, 2015; Crisp et al., 2019; Hall & Hall, 2021), wisdom (McLaughlin & McMinn, 2022), and even cognitive neuroscience and the church (Brown & Strawn, 2012; Strawn & Brown, 2020).

WHAT IS MISSING?

In this complex and vibrant landscape of integration, we may find ourselves more confused than we would have hoped. We are more informed about the theoretical and philosophical concerns of integration. We have specific models that can scaffold our approach, and we are even equipped with various "Christian" techniques in our clinical tool belt. Yet, for several reasons, as integrative clinicians deeply immersed in training and practice, we find ourselves (and our students) dissatisfied.

To clarify our position, we believe the first-wave integrationists have thoroughly justified the integration project. Even though some writers (Jeeves & Ludwig, 2018; Johnson, 2010) may chafe at the moniker *integration*, they do not argue that psychology and Christianity should remain isolated—some level of constructive dialogue is the well-accepted norm.[2] But this wave was always a launch program meant to encourage future generations; it was not intended to be the last word.

Next, while the modeling wave was a tremendous step forward in expanding the options for how we might think about an integrative dialogue, we find it limiting in two ways. First, although models of integration are important when talking about the big ideas critical to understanding Christianity and psychology, they are often far removed from the clinical dialogue. Experience-distant concepts found in theory building and theology often do not

---

[2] We do not naively ignore the fact that there are still some theological and cultural traditions where the apologetic wave is still necessary; however, this is not the central focus of this book. We are thankful for those thinkers, writers, and clinicians who are doing work to make ongoing inroads in these particular cultural and theological areas.

translate well into clear actions in the complex and dynamic practice of psychotherapy.

Second, models, inasmuch as they illuminate a path for thinking, are constrained by the assumptions of the model. Clinical material is seen through the lens of a given perspective, but rarely is the engagement reciprocal, where clinical material is allowed to shape or even influence the construction of the integrative view.[3] Moreover, these models typically assume a singular Christian worldview absent any reference to how specific Christian traditions or the social location of counselor and client may shape an integrative model and its application to the clinical environment (Strawn et al., 2014).

In a growing body of literature, researchers have attempted to develop empirically validated clinical interventions to increase religious virtues such as forgiveness, humility, gratitude, and love. With the development of positive psychology, what used to be a niche preoccupation of Christian psychologists at primarily Christian institutions is now a broad and dynamic area of intellectual and professional inquiry. Some have even called for the establishment of special competencies for those interested in clinical work that involves religious and spiritual concerns (Hathaway, 2011). Due to many shifts in both evangelical Christian culture and the discipline of psychology, we are currently witnessing an upsurge in the number of books and articles attempting to practically discuss how clinicians might apply their faith in a clinical setting or deal with specifically religious clients. For example, there are publications that explore spirituality-oriented interventions within clinical practice and evidenced-based practices that incorporate a

---

[3]Warren Brown's (2004) resonance model of integration may be an exception. While it is not a clinical model, one of its domains of knowledge—that is, experience—could be conceived of as clinical experience, and each domain is allowed to affect the integrative task.

spiritual or spiritually sensitive orientation. There are also integrative approaches to couple and marital work as well as group interventions and addiction programs. Adjunctive techniques such as spiritual journaling, Christian approaches to mindfulness, and spiritual formation processes in therapy also currently exist. What's more, exclusively Christian publishing groups are no longer the only ones producing work in this area. The American Psychological Association and other publishers are expanding the dimensions of this engagement (Aten et al., 2011; Sandage & Strawn, 2022).

While we are excited about the level of scientific rigor currently being applied to the validation of treatments sympathetic to the integration of Christian faith and psychology, as well as the prolific research on Christian virtues, we are left with a landscape similar to the Wild West. Absent a normative coherence apart from a general allegiance to Christian sensibilities and the thin ethic of modern scientific psychology, clinicians, especially students in training, face a clinical labyrinth when approaching the topic of clinical integrative practice. The complicated maze of clinical ideas and approaches is often confusing and at times tortuous, leaving many to tune a deaf ear and resort to intuition, expedient pragmatics, and collegial advice when attempting to use specific clinical approaches or techniques that might be considered integrative.

However, even if the term *integration* has become problematic for some and completely dismissed by others (Jeeves & Ludwig, 2018), we continue to find it useful. We use the term *integration* to describe an overarching project in which there are numerous methodologies/viewpoints or models. We offer this as a *hermeneutic of hospitality* that allows for different emphases, approaches, methodologies, and foci, including but not limited to particular issues of diversity. For example, we would recognize all five views in Eric Johnson's (2010) *Psychology and Christianity: Five Views* as *methodologies* of integration. We would conceptualize non-tradition-specific forms of spiritually integrated therapy also as integration (e.g., Pargament, 2011; Pargament & Exline, 2022; Griffith & Griffith, 2002; Sperry, 2012). And in certain ways we would also conceptualize the research done in the psychology of religion as a form of integration, while recognizing its limitations in terms of theological contextualization.

WHAT WE MEAN BY *INTEGRATION*

As mentioned above, the term *integration* has suffered in part due to the elastic way it has been used. As noted, it has been used to describe everything from the psychological science of studying Christian constructs to the integration of psychotherapy theory and spiritual formation. It has been stretched to the breaking point. No one term can bear that much weight or cover such diverse terrain. Out of frustration, as we indicated earlier, some have advocated giving it up. Rather than disposing of the term, however, we argue for greater specificity in its use. We think integration will benefit by articulating which psychology (which subdiscipline in psychology) and which theology (which theological tradition) are in dialogue. Integration cannot mean the same thing or look the same way when conducting empirical studies on religion as it does when working clinically with faith issues.[4] *There can be no grand unified theory of integration.* We argue that clinical integrative practice must be more specific, more process oriented, and more contextualized. Even with all the necessary specificity and complexity, integration *matters*, and in this book we will offer specific areas of reflection that matter to the overall process of clinical integration.

---

[4]In this sense we share some affinity with Hathaway and Yarhouse (2021) and their idea of domain-specific integration.

Before elucidating our contextual process model of clinical integration, we must first clarify our conceptual view of *integrative thinking*. We are guided by three process models of integration: Warren Brown's (2004) resonance model, Alvin Dueck's (2002) cultural linguistic model, and Steven Sandage and Jeannine Brown's (2018) relational model. As noted above, there is a difference between models that describe *what* integration is and models that describe *how* or the *process* of integration. These three models are dialogical in nature, engaging with numerous conversation partners that are all in play simultaneously: theology, psychotherapy (theories and empirical work), and client and therapist/counselor.[5]

Brown's (2004) resonance model, which emerges from a Wesleyan theological perspective and uses, with modifications, the Wesleyan quadrilateral, is particularly helpful when thinking conceptually about the integration of multiple epistemologies. Brown suggests that integration is ultimately an attempt to illuminate truth, and in doing so one should use five domains of knowledge: science, reason, experience, Scripture, and tradition. (1) Science is the domain of empiricism, and here the integrator uses both traditional academic research methods and the canon of empirical findings. (2) Reason is the domain of philosophy and logic. (3) Experience is both our direct personal experiences and the experientially accumulated wisdom of a community (e.g., Proverbs or accepted clinical wisdom). (4) Scripture is the holy texts of a given faith and its particular hermeneutic for interpretating those texts. Finally, (5) tradition is the historical accumulated wisdom, practices, and held knowledge of a given theological community.

---

[5] We'd also like to acknowledge Neff and McMinn's (2020) important work on embodying integration. We experience high levels of resonance between our approach and their emphasis on the dialogical nature of learning integration.

Brown (2004) suggests that when these sources of knowledge find synchrony with one another, truth becomes clearer. When there is ongoing confusion, desynchrony is implied. Integrators must return to the individual domains to fine-tune their interpretation until synchrony is achieved. Brown notes that not all domains have equal input on all truth claims. For example, the Bible has little to say about neuroscience, while neuroscience has little to say about morality. This model is respectful, as each domain retains its own integrity; it is not collapsed or reduced into any of the others, and the interactive impact of the process creates opportunities for fine-tuning or reinterpretation in each domain. Brown's model allows us to put our clinical theory and science into dialogue with Scripture, theological tradition, reason, and experience in a manner in which these are not incompatible but cooperative. This model is collaborative, as synchrony does not equate to sameness or the absence of tension, mystery, or uncertainty. It also doesn't mean the absence of conflict or times of confusion in the process of clinical work. Rather, synchrony allows for a complex engagement of information from multiple dimensions of experience, which allows for flexibility and responsiveness to the uniqueness of each clinical situation.

Second, our integrative approach engages Dueck's (2002; Dueck & Reimer, 2009) cultural linguistic model of integration, which is a culturally informed model. Dueck suggests that the disciplines of theology and psychology be conceptualized as cultural languages. As with any language or culture, each has its own semantics, syntax, norms, customs, practices, and even jokes. To become a proficient integrator is to become bilingual as well as a kind of cultural anthropologist. The goal is not to make one new, hybrid language, or to force one culture to submit to the other, but to engage in a dialogical process in which both may be truly affected.

This requires the integrator to embrace code-switching (adjusting one's behavior to fit the context of the other). Like Brown's model, Dueck's upholds the integrity of each discipline while pressing the integrator to look deeply into context in the same manner as one doing crosscultural investigations. For Dueck, there is neither solely one psychology nor one Christianity.

Finally, this leads us to Sandage and Brown's (2018) relational model of integration. These authors first remind us that disciplines don't integrate; people do. For this reason, they base their model on a differentiated relational framework. In order for effective integration to occur, integrators high in self-differentiation are clear about their own selves, their disciplines, and the limitations of both.[6] Integrative work, which they conceptualize as interdisciplinary work, naturally raises anxiety as psychologists and theologians will recognize the limits of their respective knowledge in their own and the other discipline, and may feel anxious and even ashamed for what they don't know. A self-differentiated integrator will hold on to herself in the midst of this anxiety, respecting the other, not collapsing categories, not overreaching with their discipline, and avoiding defensiveness when challenged. They liken this to intercultural competence and humility, in which one faces differentness without anxiety or defensiveness. In other words, integration requires a secure sense of self.

At first glance it may feel confusing to engage multiple models when conceptualizing integration, but we believe this speaks to the complexity of the task. Brown's (2004) model provides a heuristic

---

[6]Sandage and Brown (2018) define differentiation of self as the capacity to integrate one's personal thoughts and feelings, and manage intimacy and autonomy in interpersonal relationships. Because integration is a relational process involving persons operating from places of difference (i.e., disciplines), conflict is inevitable. Integrators with high levels of self-differentiation will neither deny difference nor make it the main focus. The self-differentiated integrator will be able to manage the anxiety of these conflicts related to difference through balancing thinking and feeling as well as intimacy and autonomy.

of how the five domains might interact (i.e., integrate) when searching for truth. The approach clarifies that our interpretations of these domains inevitably and necessarily interact. While each domain maintains its own methodology and expertise, it is through the reciprocal influence of the domains where the pursuit of truth occurs.

Dueck's cultural model reminds us of the uniqueness of each discipline and, most importantly to us, to avoid the colonialism in which one discipline usurps the other, engaging in a kind of cultural violence. It also reminds us that disciplined disciplinary competence is the goal.

Finally, Sandage and Brown's (2018) model pushes us to consider ourselves in the integrative process. While other authors have pointed out the importance of the person of the integrator, usually this is related to one's spiritual maturity (Coe & Hall, 2010). Sandage and Brown advocate a psychological model of self-differentiation of the integrator. Integration will be greatly hampered (conceptually and clinically) if the integrator is overly anxious or defensive. She must work to develop a secure sense of self, which includes ownership of her expertise and of her limitations and social location. Self-differentiated integrators will be equipped to manage their anxiety and defensiveness rather than collapsing into either-or thinking, pathologizing those who are different, and shutting down what might be ultimately a constructive conflict.

Again, we believe that these three models are process models of integration directly bearing on clinical integrative practice. They don't just tell us *what* integration does or looks like but actually make suggestions for how to go about it in the clinical room. Integration, even clinical integration, will not be able to fully escape some form of model work. Yet we hope to demonstrate a way of thinking that incorporates how-to aspects, deeply respects both disciplines, sees the personhood of the integrator and client as paramount, and gives enough freedom to engage in all the various intersectional complexities at work in the room (e.g., culture, race, nationality, different religious backgrounds, gender, sexual orientation).

WAVE FIVE: CLINICAL INTEGRATION

With all the above in place, the focus of this book is on what we refer to as *clinical integrative practice*, by which we simply mean all that occurs *in* the clinical encounter when religious faith is considered. This rather large pseudo-definition is purposefully broad for reasons we hope will become clear. It is broad because we don't want to prescribe integration or reduce it. In this sense we follow thinkers such as Siang-Yang Tan (1996), who suggests that integration can be implicit or explicit. For Tan, in implicit integration, the therapist's religious commitments inform their work in offline ways. For example, a clinician may pray silently for clients during or in between sessions, but faith, holy texts, and so on are not discussed overtly. In explicit integration, the therapist and client overtly discuss religion, faith practices, and important resources from their faith tradition, which may be helpful or may have been hurtful. We agree with Tan that explicit and implicit forms are not mutually exclusive. Therapy may move back and forth between explicit and implicit integration following the lead of the client, the clinical process of the session, and/or personal preferences of the counselor.

However, we would expand Tan's discussion by suggesting that implicit integration processes also operate unconsciously, beyond unspoken or unreported ways the therapist or counselor thinks about the client during or between sessions. We will talk more about this in the proceeding chapters, but we believe the implicit/

unconscious way integration influences our clinical work is a powerful, often unacknowledged process that may take time to enter awareness, for both therapist and client. For instance, why do therapists or counselors find themselves praying (e.g., silently in session or between sessions) for some clients and not others? If a therapist is praying for the client, does the client have a right to know? Why would this be a secret? Why do spiritual themes or ideas come to mind at one point in a session or treatment and not earlier, later, or not at all? Clearly, we can see that the process of spiritual or religious material entering the conscious deliberation of the therapy participants is multidetermined and complex.

In contrast, we are *not* advocating that integration is a kind of biblical counseling (Adams, 1970; Powlison, 2010), where the Bible (as much as we value it) is the main or only source of knowledge and intervention. Neither are we advocating for a kind of therapy in which religious resources *must* be used, invoked, or even discussed. There are many settings where religious therapists practice that do not allow for explicit integration, but as we hinted at previously, we adamantly believe that this does not mean integration is not going on.[7] As Christians in the Wesleyan tradition, we believe that God's Spirit is always at work in the world, wooing creation to God's self in both secular and religious settings.

OUR APPROACH

So, let us put our cards on the table. We advocate for integrative clinical practice not as a classic *what* model, an outcome, or even a process but as an *emergent* property. *In other words, integration emerges out of the nonlinear complex dynamic system that is the*

---

[7]We believe, as many now do, that religion must be understood as inextricably entangled with culture. In this sense it would be unethical to not allow the discussion of religion in therapy in the same way that it would be unethical to ignore culture, gender, or sexual orientation.

specific configuration of a unique therapist and client dyad. That is, something uniquely integrative (i.e., religious, spiritual) occurs within and because of the particularities of the client-therapist relationship and cannot be prescribed or reduced to something as simple as an intervention. This means that a therapist or counselor *can't* predict what integration is or what it will look like before it is experienced within the integrative moment. Neither can a therapist decide a priori what is a satisfactory integrative outcome.

What integrative clinicians *can* do is place themselves in the complex therapeutic environment in which integration may emerge. *We believe clinicians can develop sensibilities that are receptive to integrative moments.*[8] In this sense we find great affinity with Kenneth Pargament's (2011) spiritually integrated therapy (SIT). Pargament is clear that SIT is not a model of therapy but a way of being with a client such that spirituality may be included in the work. His approach, like ours, can be used with many different types of therapy models and theoretical orientations. It primarily calls for a certain kind of openness and, as we noted above, a dynamic system. In addition, we see the clinician's theory as constructive in the integrative process. For example, those who subscribe to a more cognitive-behavioral model will experience integrative moments of a different quality from those who lean toward a more psychoanalytic or systems perspective.

What do we mean by a *nonlinear complex dynamic system* and a *complex-enough environment*? Complex dynamic systems theory is a way to understand how exceedingly complex capacities (such as human development, mind, personality, relationality, spirituality,

---

[8]Our use of the term *integrative moment* is an allusion to, and in the spirit of, the work of developmental psychologist/psychoanalyst Daniel Stern (2004), who suggested the critical value of present moments in clinical work, as well as the Boston Change Process Study Group (2010), who highlighted the idea of moments of meeting as critical to therapeutic action, progress, and change.

or in our case integration) can emerge from the myriad ongoing interactions of highly complex systems (Thelen & Smith, 1994). Brains, ant colonies, economics, biological organisms, and human societies are all good examples of nonlinear dynamic systems from which new properties emerge. We conceptualize integration in the clinical practice setting emerging not from a specific way of doing something (e.g., a model), nor from invoking God's name and spirituality into the room (this would be like saying that thinking emerges from a single neuron). We believe integration emerges through the complex relationship of client and therapist intertwined in numerous and varied interactions (in both conscious and unconscious embodied ways). Even clearly explicit attempts by a therapist to invoke spiritual practices or conversations in a session cannot be fully scripted but may emerge from the way the client responds to the therapist's initiation.

Complex dynamic systems theory explains how new capacities emerge. Complex systems are self-organizing and context dependent. They are sensitive to ongoing feedback from internal and external input, allowing them to reorganize when faced with new experiences that threaten the equilibrium of the system (in dynamic systems theory these are called "catastrophes" or perturbations). For example, human persons are complex dynamic systems capable of self-organizing, which means they too can reorganize in the face of new input (this reorganization is a potential, not a given). However, because complex systems self-organize in dynamic ways, different components of the system act, create, and influence other components of the system to experience different states such as symmetry, confusion, stability, reorganization, and the like. For example, in human development we now know that infants are not passive respondents to the parent's care but actively cocreate, albeit with less sophisticated means, the caretaking environment as parent and infant teach each other and shape the nature of the relationship. The form of this relationship cannot be predicted ahead of time except in broad categories that say little about the specific characteristics of a given parent-child relationship. Change in complex systems is discontinuous, context dependent, jerky, and unpredictable (Weisel-Barth, 2006). Just like a parent-infant or any other human engagement, therapy relationships are created in the meeting of client and therapist. The developmental trajectory of this relationship and what emerges from this relationship are bounded by various contextual factors but are not predictable in specific ways.

Our above assumption that clinical integrative moments emerge and cannot be predicted, scripted, or modeled out may feel discouraging and even overwhelming. If you are a student at an integrative psychology, marriage and family, or counseling program, you have spent money and time and chosen your school, we suspect, to help you integrate. If you are a clinician who has bought this book, you were expecting some answers or at least some help. We encourage you not to despair. Not only do we believe that this way of experiencing clinical work will lead to more meaningful client-specific integrative moments, but we also believe there are practical ways to assist with this. This brings us back to complex systems. The degree to which emerging integrative moments come to fruition and affect the treatment in meaningful ways will depend on creating a *complex-enough* system. How do we develop, as noted above, the sensibilities for this kind of emergence to occur and to be noted by the therapeutic dyad?

Analogy from spiritual development. Here we draw on an analogy from the realm of spirituality. It is commonly accepted that one can't create or force spiritual experiences to occur. Rather, a spiritual seeker places oneself in a context in which spirituality might naturally emerge. This is often accomplished by placing oneself in a particular type of *setting* (e.g., church or retreat setting, place of solitude) and engaging in particular types of exercises or *practices* (again, these may be communal or solitary, but their aim is to be attuned to the moving of the Spirit). All of this is undergirded by a particular type of *mindset* (i.e., a belief that the above is facilitative of spirituality, a general openness).[9] These *settings*, *practices*, and *mindset*, cooperating with the Spirit of God and the complexity of the human person, allow for the possibility for something spiritual to emerge.

We contend that psychotherapy or counseling, with its attendant *setting, practices*, and therapist *mindset*, may (or may not) create a *complex-enough environment* for the emergence of something spiritual and integrative to occur. When it comes to the practice of psychotherapy and counseling, we believe the first two necessary elements, setting and practices, are already in place. The third element, mindset, we believe needs some further elaboration. We contend that five domains of knowledge may inform the therapist's mindset and keep him *thinking integratively*.[10] This is the development of a certain type of integrative sensibility. This is thinking integratively. This mindset, in tandem with the setting and practices of therapy/counseling, allows for maximum dynamic complexity, which is essential to the emergent integrative experience. We will have much more to say about these five domains below (each domain will have its own chapter), but for the

---

[9]It is important to note, as we will throughout the book, that we believe that all of life, cognition, affect, behavior, and even spirituality are embodied experiences. We think, feel, behave, and are spiritual in and through our bodies. Even God's Spirit is mediated to the human through our bodies. We disavow any kind of disembodied spirituality.

[10]Originally this book was to be titled *Thinking Integratively*, but we felt that this would mislead the reader that what we were suggesting was a cognitive endeavor. Rather, when we say *thinking*, we mean a completely embodied experience (including feelings and emotions), in line with the philosophers of mind who write about embodied cognition.

time being let us simply list them: hermeneutics, tradition, ethics, self-development, and resilience.

An emergent model of integration? An emergent model that is nonlinear and highly complex demonstrates that predictions, regularity, and control in therapy/counseling are illusory. We suspect that as the reader travels through this emergent *model*, they may experience a certain level of anxiety. Part of this comes from the very reason we italicize the word *model*. Models of integration tend to evoke a more static image than we intend. As mentioned above, a dynamic system is a self-organizing system. Like in human development, it may continue to evolve and move to (hopefully) higher levels of complexity and organization. When the client at the beginning of this chapter asks, "You're religious, right?" he sets in motion a process that affects the therapist and client in conscious and unconscious reciprocal ways, within the complexity of the setting and practice of the therapy. For example, as a particular integrative moment emerges from the complexity that is therapy, this new experience will have a causal impact on the therapeutic dynamic and subsequently an opportunity for continued reorganization in a kind of ongoing reciprocal feedback loop. While we believe this movement or dynamic is a much more accurate description of human persons and therapy, it can be anxiety provoking for those clinicians looking for answers on *what to do* and/or signs that they have achieved integration.

Imagine this example: You are seeing a client who has always believed that God's sovereignty means that God has complete foreknowledge of all things and subsequently has preordained all things that happen. While the client might not phrase her beliefs in quite this way, one might hear phrases such as, "All things happen for a reason" or "God is in control." When the client is faced with a personal tragedy, in complex dynamical systems language a *catastrophe*, she may either reorganize and begin to understand God's interaction in the world differently, or she may cling tightly to her familiar way of believing. If something new emerges for the client, such as, "Perhaps God doesn't cause tragedies in the world or prevent them," this new emergent idea may begin to affect other modes of inquiry, such as, "How do I understand the Bible?" and "What is the role of prayer?" The therapist and the client cannot predict ahead of time what particular integrative issues will emerge or how they will be organized consciously and unconsciously by both therapist and client.

But let us be clear: we are also *not* saying that it is the therapist's job to try to force emergence. In the above scenario, the client *may* choose to continue to believe that God has ordained all things beforehand. The therapist's job, as always, is to respect the client's particularity, which stems from their history, social location, and theological tradition. If the client chooses to continue to believe that God controls everything, it would be the therapist's responsibility to help her explore how she can or cannot accommodate the new experience (i.e., catastrophe) into her current belief system without considerable internal conflict. We will say much more about this in the coming chapters, but this is a good example of where the therapist's knowledge of their own and their client's hermeneutical way (chapter two) of seeing the world, as well as their tradition (chapter three) and ethics (chapter four), are essential in working sensitively and respectfully with clients.

These five domains (hermeneutics, tradition, ethics, self-development, resilience), which form the *mindset* of the complex dynamic system, are also useful when working with individuals who claim nominal faith, a different faith from the therapist, or no faith at all. Remember, emergence implies that one cannot decide a priori what integration will mean or look like, or where it may end up. We have both had experiences of working with clients from different faith traditions from our own who deepened in their own tradition, or working with individuals from our own faith traditions who changed or left their faith, and even individuals with little or no faith but whose needle was moved ever so slightly toward a greater faith or spirituality. From our perspective, *all* of these are emergent integrative moments.

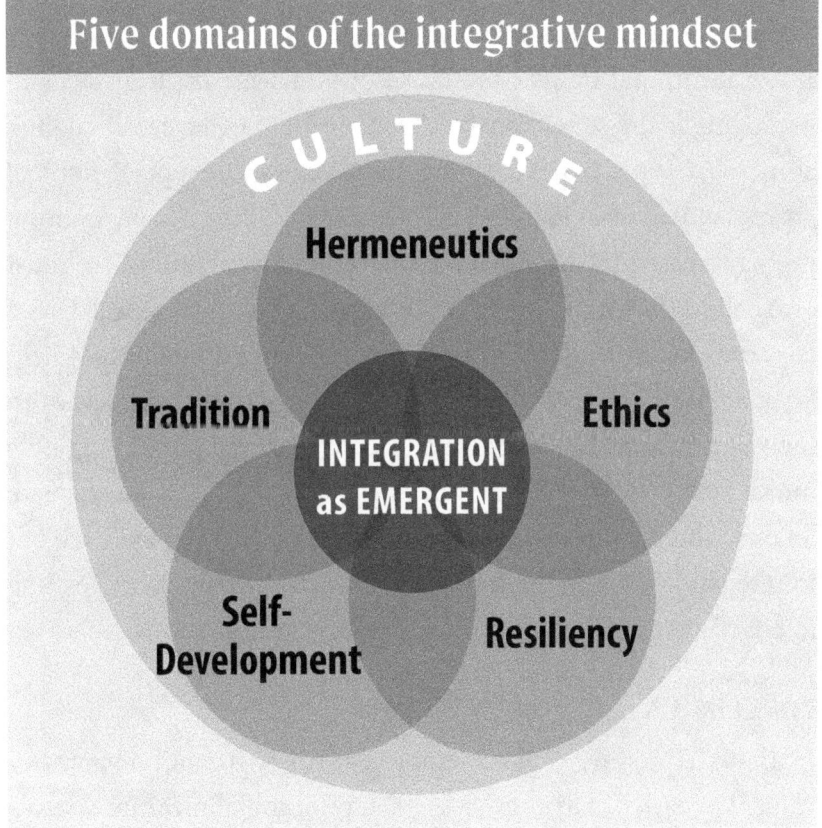

Why does this matter? We said at the outset that we hope that this book speaks to practicing clinicians and graduate students interested in the integration of clinical/counseling psychology and religious faith. We need to reiterate that we believe there are also potentially negative consequences for ignoring our proposed project. To graduate students, understandably desperate to find *the* model of clinical integration, there is a danger that you will be tempted to find a one-size-fits-all model and apply it in ways that miss the intersectional aspects of your clients (differences around religion, gender, culture, sexual orientation, etc.). While it may be hard to imagine, this is a kind of imposing or therapeutic coercion, leading not only to misunderstanding your clients but in fact doing violence to them (Dueck and Reimer, 2009).

An additional danger for those of you who are licensed and practicing is the supervisory influence you may have on fledgling clinicians. If we believe in the supervisory concept of *parallel process*, where what happens in the therapy setting can be unknowingly recreated in the supervisor setting (Sarnat, 2019), we must also believe that it can move in the opposite direction as well (from supervision to therapy). Awareness of these five domains may help a supervisor interested in encouraging integrative capacities in their supervisees to recognize and cultivate emerging integrative moments in the treatment. Ignoring the five domains may create an unsound integrative situation in supervision that plays itself out in untenable ways in the supervisee's work with his client, leading to enactments, stalemates, and premature terminations.

CONCLUSION

In this chapter we have attempted to describe our *integrative clinical perspective* as a process of developing clinical integrative sensibilities within a complex dynamic system made up of the therapeutic setting, practices, and therapist mindset. This system further interfaces with the particularity and complexity of the unique therapist-client dyad, creating a complex-enough setting for integration to emerge. Because dynamic systems are self-organizing, what emerges cannot be predicted from the sum of the parts, reduced to a priori goals, or predicted or prescribed ahead of time. While this can be anxiety provoking, from it may emerge something holy and wholly unexpected, delightful, and even life transforming. Important in our process is the assumption that the Spirit of God is constantly and pervasively operative in our attempts to form a healing clinical relationship.

We also assume that any thinking about the integrative process and experience, whether in the form of theories, justifications, or empirical research, is susceptible to the effects of sin in a fallen world. Consequently, even in our best efforts, how we think about integration clinically is prone to error and distortion. Sincerity of belief and personal conviction are not foolproof guarantees that our integrative efforts will actually align with what God is desiring in the process of our work with clients. We say this in order to infuse a modicum of humility and wondrous expectancy into our pursuit of integrative moments rather than certitude or reliance on the power and privilege of our training and knowledge. Negative integration is a possibility; in other words, discussions and uses of spiritual or religious processes in treatment are not necessarily virtuous or enhancing of therapeutic action, growth, and progress. In clinical integrative practice disintegration is an ever-present possibility; it is important to remember that good and bad can emerge from a dynamic system.

Now we turn our attention to the five essential domains in making up the mindset of the clinical integrative practitioner. Integration matters, and these are the matters that form the mindset that may create the space for integration to emerge. We hope that as you the reader take in these matters, you will be not only better prepared to work with the client's question at the beginning of the chapter but also excited to do so.

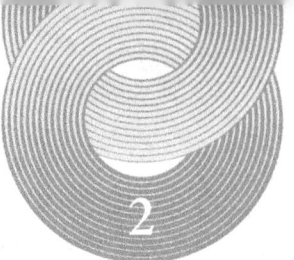

HERMENEUTICS MATTER
SETTING THE TABLE

CASE STUDY: Janis and Matthew

Janis, a thirty-five-year-old biracial female of Asian and Latina decent, had been working with Matthew, a twenty-nine-year-old biracial, cisgender male, in individual therapy for approximately eleven months. The treatment began with Mathew complaining about various states of uncertainty in his life, particularly regarding his girlfriend of four years, whom he believed was pressuring him into a greater level of commitment than he was ready to make. Other distressing issues for Matthew included his relationship with his family, his work, and his religious faith. Janis was an early-career psychologist and formed a strong working relationship with Matthew. She was well on her way to developing her own therapeutic style, and while she had been influenced by cognitive theories, emotion focused therapies (EFT), and both short- and long-term psychodynamic perspectives, for now she had settled on a depth-oriented relational-dynamic position.

Although there were many elements that made their therapeutic relationship productive, one point of mutual unease for Janis and Matthew was a transference relationship that had vague but intense qualities of attraction. Matthew would often deal with his transference anxiety by comparing Janis to his girlfriend, at times favorably and at other times not so much. Both felt a bit more comfortable when Matthew's comparison tilted toward criticizing Janis and her importance or contribution to his life and therapy. Partially this made Matthew feel more committed to his girlfriend and less needy in his relationship with Janis, while Janis felt the devaluing to be recognizable, as it aligned more with her past relationships. Being deficient in some way was an accustomed and repetitive emotional place in her family history.

Correspondingly, Janis dealt with her own ambivalent feelings of attraction to Matthew. Although she had an ongoing romantically ambiguous relationship with a long-time female partner/friend, Janis found Matthew to be "just the type of guy" that she would find appealing. His criticism of her felt safer than when he would flirt demurely by remarking how she was more attentive than his girlfriend or when he sought more personal information about her.

At one point in their work together, Matthew wanted to know more personal information about Janis, and they talked awkwardly about how this might affect their relationship. In the process Matthew became a bit frustrated with Janis regarding her lack of disclosure. He wanted more information about her thoughts and feelings, which raised significant anxiety for Janis. Was she allowed to tell him things? What if she disclosed too much? What should she do with her desire to tell him things about herself? In one session her anxiety became so intense that she lost her ability to think effectively and tried to salvage the session by defaulting to simple reflective listening.

These types of interactions were not infrequent during this phase of the treatment. They came to a head during one session when Matthew talked about how a friend had recently died by suicide, a distressing event for Mathew and his girlfriend. Matthew began talking about whether his friend, who was Christian, would go to heaven. Matthew ascribed to a broadly evangelical faith in the Reformed tradition. Janis had been raised in a somewhat stifling charismatic evangelical Christian home. In her mid-teens she and her family switched to a Reformed church, which did not loosen things up at all. As they discussed his trauma during the session, Matthew became anxious that he and Janis might not agree regarding the theological and spiritual implications of suicide.

During a supervision meeting, Janis recalled the two back-to-back sessions where the suicide was discussed. She said that Matthew was agonizing about his friend's suicide and whether Christians who died this way would go to heaven. Despite her best efforts, Matthew was not feeling adequately responded to and said to Janis, "Maybe you don't believe in truth . . . maybe we are different?" During the session Janis wanted to tell him that they actually saw things similarly, but she hesitated, not knowing whether sharing her theological understanding would be too much. Was it even ethical? She told him she felt very pulled to self-disclose. The topic shifted, and Matthew started talking about what he needed to do to in order to self-disclose more in the session. Janis responded by exploring what it meant for him to self-disclose.

As the session progressed, Matthew brought up his attraction to Janis and how it felt a little threatening to talk about. At this point Janis started to get scared in the session. Stopping her retelling of the session narrative, Janis reiterated to her supervisor how she was comfortable when clients were disappointed in her but not when they liked her. Janis then went on to recount how, as the session moved forward, Matthew said that he was worried that if Janis disclosed more about herself, his attraction would increase. As the session continued, Janis tried to empathize when

Matthew started associating to his relationship with his mother and how unknowable she was. She followed his lead but also brought up how she wanted to be very careful about disclosure because she did not want to intrude on his experience. Matthew responded, "That makes sense but feels like you are being disrespectful. What you are saying is not self-disclosure." This was near the end of the session, and Janis reported feeling awkward, foggy, and unfinished.

As she finished this session narrative, Janis reported to her supervisor that the next few days did not go well. She felt horrible most of the rest of the week, and it was very difficult for her to feel okay about her work. Was she was making progress or screwing things up? She went on to say that the next time she and Matthew met, Matthew reported that it was hard for him to come to the session. He told Janis that he had googled her and found a paper she had written on sexual identity. Inside Janis felt panic, but she tried to remain curious about Matthew's experience. She reported to her supervisor that the whole session felt shut down. Matthew stated, "It feels like you are more liberal than me," but would not elaborate his feelings. Janis felt like it was difficult to track during the session—her thinking got foggy again. At one point Matthew said, "I don't know if I'm trying to bring you back to self-disclosing or . . ."

Janis struggled to know what to say. What was she feeling? What did Matthew need? She felt increasingly lost. The session soon ended, much to Janis's relief.

INTERPRETATION AND UNDERSTANDING

There is perhaps no discipline that relies more heavily on accurate interpretation and understanding than psychotherapy and counseling. Because we move toward the one who is suffering—the client—we often must work hard to get our understanding right, to really grasp the essence of what the client is dealing with so that we may be as helpful as possible. Janis and Matthew are struggling to form a shared understanding and certainly present us with many questions and gaps as to how their therapeutic relationship is progressing. What is going on in the relationship that might be important to their work? Why is Janis unable to keep her thinking clear in the session? What is the meaning of their vague, anxiety-laden mutual attraction? Why is Matthew exploring Janis's internet profile? What does their relationship have to do with helping Matthew reach his treatment goals? What is God up to in Matthew's work with Janis, not just in Matthew's life but for Janis as well? How might Janis's professional theories and experience be influencing her, especially since she is under supervision? Why are theological issues emerging in the treatment, and how do they influence the relational dynamics? How is gender, sexuality, or race affecting their conversations?

Understanding the meaning of what is communicated between Matthew and Janis is critical for their work to progress, and determining whether they share a *correct* understanding of each other is essential. Upon reflection, we might agree that this treatment relationship has reached a high level of complexity due to the nature of the presenting problem, the length of treatment, and the intricacies of the treatment relationship. All good treatment decisions, regardless of complexity, duration, the nature of the presenting problem, and the theoretical orientation, have at their foundation the ability of the counselor and client to mutually understand what is going on and how to move forward. Yet, as anyone who has had a conversation involving intense feelings amid deep reflection knows, understanding the meaning of the other person's experiences is often no easy task. Influenced both by conscious and unconscious factors, we know that missteps and confusion are common and often require us to slow down, restate something, or ask for clarification. Despite the importance of arriving at a shared meaning or understanding, therapeutic conversations are fraught with subtleties and undercurrents that often derail understanding and short-circuit our progress to effectively meeting the client's needs and goals. If, however, as Philip Cushman (2020) argues, "the natural state of affairs in a conversation is misunderstanding" (p. 222), we must become experts at deciphering and grasping meaning before we communicate our understanding.[1]

The purpose of this chapter is to talk about how hermeneutics, the study of interpretation, is critical to clearly understand what is happening in psychotherapy and counseling. We argue that appreciating hermeneutics is essential if we are to develop a deep, rich, flexible, and practical understanding of clinical integration.[2] Using Matthew and Janis as a case example, we highlight how an appreciation of hermeneutics clarifies meaning in clinical work and helps the clinician identify how integration may emerge from within the treatment relationship. Before we jump to clinical application, however, it will be useful to think about how hermeneutics, a subject more familiar to theologians and philosophers, might be deeply relevant to psychotherapy and counseling.

Most academics who think and write about interpretation and understanding work in the area of hermeneutics, a subject that

---

[1] Here Cushman is following a long line of hermeneuticists, such as Hans-Georg Gadamer, Charles Taylor, and Clifford Geertz, who have attempted to address the structuring of interpretation and understanding in human dialogue.

[2] We acknowledge here that we are not the first or only clinicians to argue for the utility and importance of hermeneutics as a critical framework for integration. For example, William Hathaway (2002) provides a clear and compelling case for considering hermeneutics as a move "toward an expanded and richer comprehension that harmoniously synthesizes insights about the real world from both contemporary psychology and Christian thought" (p. 216). Our goal here is to focus the use of hermeneutics specifically in the clinical relationship.

speaks directly to how we come to understand the meaning of texts such as sacred Scriptures, literature, the visual arts, and, yes, other humans. At a very straightforward level, hermeneutics is about how we come to understand or interpret meaning from something that might not be clear. What rules or methods will best help us get to a meaningful understanding? Let's take an example from poetry.

> ***This is just to say***
> I have eaten
> the plums
> that were in
> the icebox
> and which
> you were probably
> saving
> for breakfast
> Forgive me
> they were delicious
> so sweet
> and so cold

William Carlos Williams (1938), known for his clear and vivid writing, sets before us a poem we can immediately grasp. There is no mystification, no words we need to untangle. Lacking pretext, it lays naked for us the meaning: someone took the favored plums from the icebox and now, perhaps feeling guilty, has left a note to apologize. Pretty straightforward, no grand interpretation needed, some might say. But is this entirely correct? What if we pause a little and think about how, in response to the poem, we begin to build associations from our own experience? Perhaps we have encountered something similar—a lost meal or something we thought was waiting for us in the refrigerator, and alas, when we got home it was missing. Perhaps we don't like plums, and our association is indifference. Perhaps it raises a sense of injustice—how could he? Or a tinge of mirth, what the Germans call schadenfreude—glee or pleasure of another's misfortune.

Whatever the response, we can see that the poem is not really experienced at face value. We bring countless associations from our own lived contexts to something that seems simple. We may even reflect on the author's intent in writing the poem as our meaning making engages the discovery of him as a person, the social and cultural context of his work, and his literary style. This is a process of interpretation; the very act of making sense of the poem involves meaning making, in this case mostly from our own personal experience.

Let's take one more example, an excerpt from a work by Korean poet Yun Dong-ju (2003):

A Poem That Came Easily
The night rain whispers outside the window
Of my six-mat room, in an alien country.
The poet has a sad vocation I know:
should I write another line of poetry?
Having received my tuition from home in an envelope
soaked with the smell of sweat and love,
I tuck my college notebook under my arm
I go off to listen to the lecture of an old professor.
Looking back, I see that I have lost my childhood friends:
one and two at a time—all of them.
What was it that I was hoping for,
and why am I simply sinking to the bottom alone?
Life is meant to be difficult:
it is too bad
that a poem comes so easily to me.

Half a world away, Yun, a contemporary of Williams, despite his markedly melancholic tone, strikes a similar vein with his forthright language, clear imagery, and the absence of bewildering metaphors. While we might wonder a bit more about the nature of Yun's experience—why was he in an alien country? how and why did he lose his friends?—the sense of his poem comes through clearly. The language does not seem to be in need of deep interpretation as, again, we associate to the poem from our own experience. What are our experiences of being away from home? Have we ever sent our child money at college or received money from home as a college student? The notebook, the old professor, the lost childhood friends—all these images conspire with our lives, our lived context, to help us draw meaning from the poem. By *meaning*, however, we are not necessarily referring to some overarching moral or insight. This may be something that develops, but mostly we initially respond with impressions or feelings. Think about how we make sense of the poem as we draw from our own experience—the way we associate the thought of being away from home.

Pausing here for a moment, we want to highlight something that is critical in our discussion of hermeneutics and clinical work: the constant need for a self-reflective stance. For example, in our previous suggestion about where to focus our thoughts as we read the poem, we suggested a very particular starting point, tuning to our emotional experience or personal memory. Yet this is only one approach we could take. If we were literature professors or sociologists and not psychologists and counselors, we might suggest a different starting point, such as the analysis of language or the use of cultural categories. The starting points and methods of hermeneutics have long been debated, and there continues to be deliberation and preferences about what is the most appropriate.

For our purposes, because we are clinicians, we are not saying affective experience is the only starting point for interpretation, but it is certainly a critical one if we are to effectively deal with our client's suffering. More importantly, however, we are championing the need to reflectively acknowledge and consider, to the degree we can, the impact of the place from where we start our hermeneutical process. We have known for some time now that both implicit and explicit affective or emotional processing is deeply shaped and organized by our developmental experience and context. Lynne Layton (2004) uses the term *normative unconscious* to talk about how culture, gender, race, ethnicity, religion—the situation of our birth, so to speak—is constantly shaping our organization of the world, including the structure and texture of presumptions, expectations, and beliefs. Even though we mature into more sophisticated conscious acknowledgment of these shaping influences, what we automatically interpret as *normal* in our everyday living, and the categories available to us to organize our interpretive process, is deeply structured by our personal experience of, and in, our particular social location. A great example of this is seen in Marie Hoffman's (2016) work exploring the intergenerational traumatic precursors to the formation of dispensational theology.

At this point you may be wondering: Fair enough, but how do I know whether my interpretation, my understanding of the poem, is correct? Even in these relatively forthright poems, how do we know that our perspective isn't mere opinion? What if I'm wrong? What is the truth of the matter? The anxiety around truth and meaning is important. We will weave in and out of this critical aspect of hermeneutics as we progress and we speak directly to the notion of integrative truth toward the end of the chapter. Suffice it to say here that some have suggested that the way to tackle the question of *correctness* is to probe the historical setting and the psychological character or disposition of the author. In doing so, we are more likely to understand what the author intended.

Whether this leads us to the *truth* of the poem is debatable, but let's proceed. Does it help, for instance, to know that Yun was Korean and lived his whole life under Japanese colonial occupation? In 1942, when he wrote this poem, World War II was raging, and he was studying in Kyoto, Japan. The next year he was arrested for allegedly participating in the resistance movement, and he died in prison at age twenty-seven, six months before Korea declared its independence from Japan in 1945. When he speaks of the alien country, he is probably talking about his oppressors. Childhood friends were not lost to time but were actually lost to violence and political oppression.

Knowing the background of Yun helps to thicken the meaning of his poem. Now, not only do we have our own personal thoughts and feelings, but these are mingled with our knowledge of Yun's plight. This allows us to expand our understanding and grasp more complex meaning from his poem. If we were to go back and reread the poem at this point, we would see that our understanding has shifted, expanded, and perhaps become infused with more nuanced emotions or assumptions. Further, if we understand that Yun's poem is a translation from Korean, how does this affect our meaning-making process? What does it mean to read this poem in a different cultural context or from the gaze of a different race or ethnic position? Deeply embedded in both conscious/explicit and unconscious/implicit processing are cultural assumptions that powerfully and inextricably shape any meaning-making process. Hermeneutics is not separate from culture, race, gender, sexuality, ability, or other categories of difference; these distinctives are fundamentally entangled and embodied in the process of our meaning making. As Robert Stolorow (2013) says (nuancing a Gadamerian perspective to clinical work)—we have no "immaculate perception" (p. 384)—the very nature of our interpretation betrays our situatedness, our place in the world.

THE HERMENEUTICAL CIRCLE

This process of increasing our understanding of something when we gain more knowledge is what philosophers Fredrick Schleiermacher and, later, Martin Heidegger referred to as the *hermeneutical circle*. Essentially our thoughts or interpretations about meaning are continually being upgraded, deepened, and made more complex as we gain more information about the text we are reading. We see here that the *true meaning* of something may be open to evolution as our exposure and understanding increase. Simply put, the more we read a text, or other sources that are commenting on a text, the thicker our understanding becomes, and this understanding informs how we engage the text moving forward. This same process is evident when we seek understanding of art in all its forms. Still, you may be saying that this does not erase doubt regarding the truth of our interpretation with any degree of certitude. Maybe, but let's keep going and see whether there are ways to think about this that might help us arrive at a comfortable degree of certainty.

Let's pivot now as we return to thinking about Janis and Matthew. If we move from the humanities, which are largely preoccupied with actual texts and images, how might we think about the complexity of human conversation, with all its attendant contextual influences and the intricacy of conscious and unconscious determinants in light of hermeneutics? After all, Janis and Matthew are interpreting each other constantly, and we as distal observers are interpreting the meaning and purpose of their relationship and actions as well. Many have argued that one of the most fundamental capacities of human psychological functioning is the inescapable interpretive nature of our thoughts and emotions. In other words, as Hans-Georg Gadamer (1975) has so aptly demonstrated, we are never not interpreting, and when seeking meaning we are never not operating hermeneutically.

Therefore, as we think about this case as integrative clinicians, our focus on hermeneutics is not an attempt at a theory or model of integration, but rather we seek to describe a set of practical ways to contemplate the clinical encounter as a Christian clinician. We are not pursuing a theory of how to integrate but want to deepen our capacities to recognize integrative experiences and moments when they emerge within the clinical relationship. This approach, no doubt, contains assumptions about the nature of therapeutic and divine action (something we describe in earlier writings; see Bland & Strawn, 2014; Brown & Strawn, 2012), which we see as inextricably entangled within the relationship forged between the client and the therapist or counselor.

As we stated in chapter one, unlike previous integrative discussions, we do not want to structure or define integration so much as to deepen our experience of integrative moments and provide a way of thinking and talking about how integration emerges within the relationships we form with clients. Taking a cue from Gadamer (1975) about the importance of understanding, we want to respect the sacredness of the clinical relationship and the therapeutic process as a domain of God's healing presence regardless of whether the religious allegiances held by each participant are acknowledged. Our approach is a deeply experiential way to inhabit integration. Understanding clinical integration belongs to the encounter between client and counselor. Therefore, when we seek to recognize, discover, and think about the practical ways to organize experience so that we can identify God's work in our work, we can reflect as we ask, "What is God up to?"

Necessarily, then, this will involve paying close attention to the many ways our thoughts and emotions, in all their complex arrangement, are shaped and influenced by our clinical work—and the specific way these emotions and thoughts are uniquely organized depending on the specific clients we see. If, as we are assuming, understanding is of supreme value in the therapeutic relationship, and, at least for now, we accept that hermeneutics is a critical factor in the articulation of this understanding, we want to consider two questions in the remaining pages of this chapter that speak to exactly which aspects of hermeneutics matter most for our integrative process.

The first critical element involves how we establish a clinically integrative mindset; in other words, what do we need to consider when engaging in the process of understanding integrative moments? Second, what do we need to consider to establish some sense of confidence that our understanding is in the ballpark of what is really going on and that our participation in integrative clinical practice is helpful and healing for our clients?

We will conclude this discussion by giving a brief outline of the different domains of our clinical experience that shape the content of our integrative moments. We begin with a conversation about understanding because our assumption is that hermeneutics, as Gadamer (1975) says, is *propaedeutic*, or serves as an introduction to understanding; and, in our thinking, robust clinical integration is impossible without first attending to the nature of clinical hermeneutics.

ESTABLISHING A MINDSET FOR UNDERSTANDING

One of the assumptions of a hermeneutical approach to therapy and counseling is that the rules or expectations of therapy can be applied only starting from the abstract. Because no one can predict the specifics of any clinical encounter with absolute accuracy, all theory application is necessarily an abstract approximation mediated through the person of the therapist. We've all been in situations either in graduate school or continuing education where the presentation of a therapeutic approach, technique, or intervention works great in the case presented. Or maybe we read research that shows a manualized or specific approach demonstrating high levels of success with a certain population. Inspired, we sometimes leave these classes or seminars hyped up to tackle our own clinical population by applying our newfound knowledge—often with mixed or even disastrous effects. We know our new ideas conceptually but have not yet experienced their efficacy in a real encounter with a complex human.

Situations like this are why we regularly refer to counseling as an art, one that takes mentorship, supervision, and accumulated understanding. Hopefully the gradual accumulation of real-world experience allows us to gain what Michael Polanyi (1958) referred to as tacit knowledge or expertise—the type of knowledge you acquire just by doing and hanging around, talking to, and watching other doers. This real-time proficiency allows you to decipher the practicality of a given approach or theoretical idea/intervention while working with *your* client. This is one of the reasons even the most strictly manualized treatments are most effective when the practicing therapists go off script a little, or even a lot, to adapt to the demands of a given clinical relationship (Norcross et al., 2006).

When thinking about integration in the case of Janis and Matthew, deciding how to respond to the suicide of Matthew's friend—a tragedy likely to evoke religious or spiritual associations (thoughts and emotional responses)—will be shaped by the collision of the existing knowledge and experience of God/theology/Christian culture of each individual involved in the conversation.

(We discuss these Christian cultures, or what we call traditions, in the next chapter.) In fact, the specific case of Matthew and Janis will animate spiritual and theological possibilities that could only emerge from their unique therapeutic relationship. Not to lean too sharply into a Wesleyan theological sensibility here, but in psychotherapy the affective experience of one's theology and Christian life is critical for considering the nature of each integrative moment. Psychotherapy and counseling are nothing if not drenched in affective possibility. While abstract discussions of theology or religious topics may be attempted, they take meaning only within the specific emotional context of the therapy relationship. In other words, *what is God up to* in this emotionally engaged relationship at this time? That is the integrative moment.

THE EXPERIENCE OF CLINICAL INTEGRATION

Consequently, an extension of our approach is that clinical integration is always *experience near*. It cannot be abstract or modeled but instead must be closely tracked as it is realized in the relational experience. In our work as integrative clinicians, along with providing a justification or apology for the integrative project, we have consistently introduced our students and supervisees to the different models of integration (see our discussion of the waves of integration in chapter one). For instance, one helpful clinical contribution to the modeling wave is Stephen Greggo and Timothy Sisemore's (2012) work *Counseling and Christianity: Five Approaches*, which attempts to bring some of these models into practical focus. Leading their discussion is a consideration of the individuality of the counselor and the importance of self-knowledge. In the subsequent chapters, highly experienced clinicians attempt to lay out how these different models might be applied in the clinical relationship. Each subsequent discussion is engaging and thoughtful, and gives an example of each author's sincere attempt to actualize the model.

While we find the clinical discussion fascinating, we are less enthusiastic about it as a definitively clear representation of the abstracted model. In other words, we find the chapters to be more a reflection of the individuality of each writer's understanding of the approach to clinical integration than an articulation of the specific ways in which the model should or could be expressed clinically. Our very use of the word *should* in the last sentence gives evidence to the powerful forces at work that shape the specific expression of any idea within the clinical exchange. We believe this is an unfortunate, mostly implicit implication of abstract models or theories. Theoretical ideas about clinical approaches have a way of setting up subtle expectations that there is a right or wrong way to apply the model or theory. This makes sense when we are talking about broad categories such as practicing a Christian integrative approach rather than an Islamic integrative approach (e.g., Abu-Raiya, 2015), but it gets more complicated when we are talking about more nuanced expressions of how differing perspectives on Christianity affect clinical work. For example, if we choose the integrative model as opposed to the Christian psychology model (see Johnson 2010; Greggo & Sisemore, 2012), wouldn't these each look different depending on the particularity of the faith and method of application of each given clinical encounter?

If, in fact, as we think Greggo and Sisemore would attest, there is a range of *correctness* in the way models are applied, we must attend to how a multitude of factors may shape the process of model application or integration. Further, what makes one model of integration preferable over another, except the unique conscious and unconscious preferences (hermeneutical frame) of the therapist? Is individual theological preference a sufficient justification for using a given set of ideas for the exercise of clinical integration with a given population? What does it even mean to think about better and worse approaches to integration? Our concern is *not* that the models are insufficiently complex, lack justification, or are irrelevant to clinical work; our concern is that the practical embodiment of each model reveals the conscious and unconscious preferences and prejudices/biases that lead each person to choose a particular model in the first place. These biases, if you will, form the basic hermeneutical structure for integration. In other words, deep theological and cultural preferences are always powerfully operative in the choice of one model over the other. In intellectual debates or academic readings, these preferences and biases can be abstracted and debated, but in the counseling relationship they operate practically and within experience-near engagements at multiple levels of consciousness.

For us these issues and questions are important and related to the more fundamental dimension of clinical integration. If abstract theories don't land fully within the clinical relationship, what does it mean to use an integration model as an a priori guide to shaping the clinical experience—is this even a helpful way to think about clinical integration? From the perspective of hermeneutics, no rule can fully speak to individual experience. A rule, model, or guideline cannot sufficiently comprehend an individual situation for the very reason that the individual situation amends, particularizes, co-constructs, and supplements the universal rule. All integration stories and emergent integrative moments are individual stories that link to shared communal experiences. This is why the experience of being a counselor is always a version of what you read about. It's why manualized treatments will never work optimally without the person of the therapist. It's why supervision or consultation about a case is so vital but will be limited in effectiveness unless one has time to grasp the contextual specificity of the clinical question brought to supervision.

We realize and empathize, however, that this type of thinking may make learning how to be an integrative therapist somewhat bewildering, especially for young clinicians. If there is no reliable rule or guideline telling me if I am doing what I should be doing, how do I know whether I'm doing it right? Can I overcome, as Valery Hazanov (2019) puts it, "the fear of doing nothing" (p. 1)? This is the question we hear all the time. Am I really learning how to integrate? A recent effort by Megan Neff and Mark McMinn (2020) takes this hermeneutical approach more seriously by addressing the embodied and dialogic nature of learning integration—that all integration efforts are situated in relationships and particularized by the person of the integrator. In their view, learning integration is a highly conversational endeavor. One cannot effectively apply an intellectual idea without owning the idea through relational engagement. Their work is helpful in identifying pedagogical priorities in the field of integration, and they also consider what we believe to be essential element missing in most Western discussions of integration: identifying and laying bare the fundamental organizing principles of culture, race, class, gender, and sexual orientation of the persons who are writing integration theory and models.

HESITATIONS AND QUESTIONS

Now, you may find yourself hesitating here, thinking that we are throwing all theorizing, modeling, and rules under the proverbial bus. Be assured this is not at all what we are saying. What we specifically want to communicate is that in discussions of *clinically integrative practice*, we must take the actual context of clinical work as our foundational area of application. The clinical experience is not primarily something discussed in the classroom or hypothetically in one's mind; real flesh and real bodies are engaging in the clinical exchange. The clinical relationship is irreducibly intersubjective. This means, as we have already said, the unique personhood of each therapist is critical to the flow and animation of the integration theory, model, or rule. As a side note, this person-of-the-therapist emphasis is not a particularly new discussion in integration.[3] Yet we do not mind restating and bringing to the front of the pack this critical element of clinical experience because we believe it is easily dismissed or minimized in the noise of competing clinical priorities. Different theoretical positions, the emotional tumult of treatment, and various external factors (economic and insurance realities, licensing boards, professional accreditation bodies, evidence-based treatment protocols, continuing education requirements, etc.) all exert enormous influence on practicing clinicians. All of these pressures distract us from a needed mindfulness to the way our personhood—both consciously and unconsciously—shapes integrative clinical practice.

Truth and correct understanding. A second hesitation people may have when considering hermeneutics is related to the notion of what is a true, reliable, and proper way to approach integration in our clinical work. How do we bring the declarative truth of our Christian faith into the clinical relationship in order for there to be integration? In other words, what truth is relevant to our clinical example? Is there a proper way for Janis to respond to Matthew's ideas about suicide, particularly the theological or spiritual aspect of this issue as it has emerged in the conversation?

---

[3]Coe and Hall (2010), Greggo and Sisemore (2012), Sandage and Brown (2018), and Sorenson (2004) have all alluded to or spoken directly about the importance of therapist subjectivity in the process of integration.

While we do not want to sideline ourselves with a long discussion of truth in the clinical relationship (and we've already talked about the complications when we use the word *should*), we want to acknowledge that concerns about the truthfulness of one's understanding are far from irrelevant, and this has been a major area of preoccupation and debate in the field of hermeneutics. Using the clinical setting as our exemplar to figure out the specifics, the main point of concern goes something like this: if the psychologist or counselor, who is subject to fallible thinking, is trying to understand the client, who is also subject to fallible thinking, even if she does an excellent job in understanding the client, how do we know that they are arriving at any understanding or conclusion that is true? By *true* here we mean reliable, productive, or likely to lead to a reasonably correct understanding that will foster health, growth, and virtue. Even if the therapist believes she needs to correct false understandings because she has greater experience or perceived theological accuracy, as we described earlier, what prevents us all from falling into a *vicious circle* where we keep developing more elaborate false understandings?[4]

Admittedly, there are many aspects of our clients' lives that are discussed in therapy that are not about arriving at some correct answer or belief. These issues in therapy have a range of reasonable

---

[4]It should be noted that this argument or a similar version is often touted by those who lean toward a biblical counseling integrative perspective. Their way out of the potential trap of perpetual error is to claim that Scripture is the only reliable authority on which to base a counseling relationship. While we may disagree with this claim, we do not see it as historically illegitimate. Of course, what is frequently missing or ignored in this argument is an identification of the hermeneutical approach these counselors bring to Scripture, which by extension exerts both conscious and unconscious effects on their clinical work. Therapists from this perspective frequently tilt to a more literalist or *plain-text reading* (see Johnson, 2007; Murphy, 1996), while ignoring or minimizing the impact of their own social location and subjectivity on their particular reading of Scripture. We are not making a point about the validity of this hermeneutical stance, but we would argue that not acknowledging the contextual subjectivity (Flemming, 2005) of any attempt to use the Scripture as a basis for counseling and therapy may be negligent, particularly if it ignores the relevance of therapist bias and predetermined assumptions.

understandings, and arriving at a singular truth would be ridiculous. For instance, how we understand the source of a client's anxiety will likely have a complex set of contributing and exacerbating contextual causal features. Getting at a singular truth or correct explanation is complicated and for some theories of treatment unnecessary. In fact, there are several ways to think about the truthfulness of understanding in clinical work.

One solution might be to examine the way we think about truth. For instance, sometimes it is clinically helpful to think about truth as an object, idea, or belief, and sometimes it is helpful to think about truth as a process: What is true, real, and desirable about the way we are conducting ourselves clinically and the telos of our clinical actions (Allison & Fonagy, 2016)? While this latter way of thinking about truth becomes indispensable in the clinical process for fostering a shared sense of trust and safety, both conceptualizations of truth are mutually compatible and also contestable, open to various nuances of opinion and verification. In the clinical experience, as we have discussed earlier, a distanciated view of truth—one that seeks to distance and objectify truth—is often of limited value, as we don't live our lives as objects; we live as subjects.

Now, before anyone gets anxious about abandoning truth, we are not talking about the lack of objective knowledge; we are simply highlighting that any so-called *objective truth* that is relevant to human psychological functioning has to be subjectively embodied and understood within the unique contextual domains of each therapist-client relationship. In the therapeutic relationship, language and emotion are context dependent and take on meaning within the specific possibilities or frame of the relational connection. Further, recalling Brown's resonance model, mentioned in chapter one, we know that truth of clinical experience becomes more solid to the degree that it resonates with other factors that indirectly weigh on the therapeutic experience—reason, science, tradition, and Scripture.

Clinically, we can see this anxiety about correctness and truth emerging in the experience of Janis and Matthew. If they believe different things or see things differently, are they able to continue in their relationship, and does this mean that one view is correct and the other isn't? While there are many thoughts and emotions going on in their exchange, we cannot separate the discussion regarding theological views of suicide from the conflicted feelings of attraction and what is appropriate to share between client and therapist. Not only is Janis concerned about the professional boundaries related to sharing her own views of a controversial theological topic; she also may be wondering whether it is even important to go into the theology. Is that possibly a distraction from the emotional meaning of suicide and death? In other words, is the movement to theology serving a defensive or self-protective function? But even if she decides it's not defensive and open for discussion, what is the emotional toll on the relationship if they disagree theologically? Can their relationship, which is saturated with fears and longings about intimacy and liking, tolerate differentness in this area—or sameness? Faith is important to both Janis and Matthew, and both have been influenced by rather inflexible theological systems where *right belief* is associated with who belongs and who doesn't. Perhaps even more frightening, however, is that they might see things similarly, and this would lead to a deepening or expansion of the attractive longing, "Look, we have so much in common."

One can see here that the pursuit of some abstract theological truth about the correct way to view suicide could be the least important thing to understand between Janis and Matthew. Perhaps what is truer and more correct in terms of the therapeutic and healing process—the place that God is operative—is in the working out of relational longing and the capacity of both Janis and Matthew to talk about states of attraction, similarity, difference, and so on in a manner that expands emotional and self-capacities to engage difference or similarity without creating unbearable distance or collapsing into an inappropriate expression of connection.

Part of our concern when talking about truth involves the way we are typically socialized into religious and theological conversations by our respective traditions. Learning and inhabiting a religious tradition most often involves an immersion into a thick community—a community that is mutually formed, and where the truth and experience of theological knowledge is shaped and supported within the everyday practices and liturgies of a faith tradition (see chapter three). We cannot escape the implicit way these theological *beliefs or truths* inhabit our responses to all manner of conversation, particularly those that swing toward the moral or ethical dimension of our lives (see chapter four for this discussion). Consequently, we find that the integration project, especially for those of us who subscribe to some form of Western evangelicalism, has always carried implicit, often unacknowledged, and sometimes insidious characteristics of particular agendas that emerge from this tradition and are expressed in the integration literature.

All integration stories are individual stories that link to shared communal/relational experiences. One example of this might be the tendency of some integration literature to have a missiological hue. In other words, the culture of Christianity, particularly in its evangelical expression, is drenched in theological imperatives, one of these being the Great Commission's "Therefore go and make disciples of all nations" (Matthew 28:19). Our argument is not about the validity of this imperative; certainly we believe the good news of the gospel is worth sharing. However, we also want to be scrupulously aware when these partialities, developed within our socioreligious contexts, are exerting influence within the clinical relationship. We believe this is important not so that these values (e.g., tradition and ethics; see chapters three and four) can somehow be bracketed, denied, or sanitized. Rather, because theology often acts as an unconscious organizer in our work, our beliefs should be acknowledged and owned in order to avoid speaking errantly from our own tradition without a sensitivity or recognition of the alternative perspectives/traditions that exist in our clients.

We also reject the notion promoted by much of the professional mental health community that religious values should be extracted or at the very least toned down. First, we do not believe this is possible; and second, this notion mistakenly asserts that somehow good psychotherapy or counseling occurs within a religiously antiseptic frame. We are not asserting that theology somehow takes center stage in the clinical work; we are merely affirming that, when religion or theological topics emerge within the clinical relationship, these topics and the accompanying feeling states ought not to be ignored or simply given a cursory glance, any more than we would ignore culture, race, or sexuality. If we are to be fully present and nimble therapists and counselors, we must develop clinical relational skills that can broach any topic that reasonably affects the client's emotional life and is relevant to the goals of a particular treatment. This is exactly why hermeneutics matters. Further, those of us interested in the integrative process must pay attention to the affective coloring and clinical context in which integrative themes emerge. Why now? What is the feeling or tone of the conversation? What might God be up to at this moment?

Our position is an elaboration of a perspective that has been present in other discussions of the integration of Christianity and psychology/counseling (see Jones, 1994, for a pivotal introduction).

Beyond mere conscious acknowledgment of the psychologist's faith perspective, however, we want to expand and specify the discussion, not only by emphasizing that our theological organizing principles are always operative at unconscious levels but also to hone our sensitivity to how and why these organizing principles emerge at particular times in a given treatment. We believe that unacknowledged integration material (e.g., thoughts, feelings, impressions, expectancies about faith and religion) can be quite helpful or at times harmful for the treatment. As we hinted at in chapter one, viewing integration as an emergent property essentially challenges the ubiquitous assumption that integration outcomes are always a good thing, an assumption we believe permeates the integration literature.

Perhaps, at times, when certain aspects of personal faith enter the clinical relationship, it can be limiting or even misguided, out of step with where the Spirit of God might be leading. For instance, we have often found that religious and theological assumptions have the capacity to emerge in ways that skew clinical work in the direction of privileging White Christian priorities (Joshi, 2020; McNeil, 2005). This may not be particularly problematic unless the therapist and client are unable to acknowledge and explore the meanings that arise and the significance these meanings play in the treatment relationship. Another example of negative integration may emerge when religious contexts are sources of trauma. Given that faith experiences are often saturated in value language and moral imperatives, painful emotions such as guilt, shame, grief, and feelings of exclusion or devaluation of one's worth can easily be activated when therapy touches on thoughts or feelings about religious life and practice.

If we apply these ideas to Janis and Matthew, we can see that the explicit emergence of theology and faith within their relationship occurred in the normal rhythms of treatment for good, or sometimes not so good. The expression of integrative material will consistently be colored by the relational dynamics between therapist and client. In our psychoanalytic tradition this is referred to as *transference-countertransference dynamics*, but we can also think about it in terms of the working relationship or the treatment alliance. Our focus on transference is important because it speaks to the unique contextual factors that frame any discussions of faith and theology in a psychotherapy setting. Psychotherapy is not typically associated with religious faith, and we are missing the typical meaning-making contextual cues that ordinarily frame religious discussions—think about being in church or small group Bible study.

For Janis, we can still see that the emergence of theology—what happens to a person who dies by suicide?—was deeply embedded in her concerns about the therapeutic relationship and anxiety about the ethics of her personal disclosure and what this might mean for their relationship. This anxiety would probably not have occurred had she been talking with Matthew in a more conventional religious context. Would it be dangerous to share? What does she do with her desire to be known by Matthew while contending with his ambivalence and anxiety about getting too close? How does Matthew know more about Janis and yet preserve his fidelity to his girlfriend?

At this point we might be tempted to collapse the theological issue into an emotional transference organization, which is common in mental health theory, but what happens if we see the conversation as multilayered and nuanced? An important aspect of our assumption about integration is that it is not phenomenologically separate from the experience of therapy itself. This is different from those who argue that Christian integration in psychotherapy is present only when there is an explicit acknowledgment of themes, processes, or behaviors that are overtly Christian. Think about praying in a session or for a client, or explicitly initiating a treatment protocol focused on forgiveness as a strategy to overcome loss or injury. These interventions may indeed be integrative, but if we believe God is animating the very processes of psychotherapy and counseling, clearly unconscious and preconscious organizing principles influence our integrative endeavors. We do not believe that God is only or even primarily at work, or that integration happens, only when his name is explicitly invoked (we significantly expand on this topic in chapter six).

But we've drifted a bit, perhaps, in our discussion of how we can develop the ability to become reasonably certain that our therapy and specifically our integrative efforts are emerging from a truthful process and are revealing truthful insights and emotional confidence. Let's now turn to our final topic, the role of critical thinking and distanciation. Here we hope not to alleviate all tension and anxiety of reaching truth but instead to offer a perspective we can hold securely and with humility.

Distanciation or perspective taking as a method of truth seeking. In clinical conversations about empathy, especially as new clinicians are learning how to harness their tendency to privilege their own subjective perspective, imaging oneself *in the shoes* of the client is a foundational route to understanding. Most clinicians can remember classes in graduate school aimed specifically at developing the skill of listening to a person without asking questions. Along with developing an empathic, attuned clinical relationship, which is itself therapeutic, the goal of these empathy learning exercises is not to shun questions in clinical work but to highlight how much we tend to see and interpret the world from our own perspective. Once we become aware of our overactive tendency to shape conversations according to our subjective prejudices and assumptions about the world, we are better able to listen in a manner that facilitates the unfolding of a client's story in a manner that permits understanding. While affirming that one can never escape the subjective position completely, it is reasonable to assume that we can hold a critical or distanciated perspective even about our own experience and internal emotional processing.

Distanciation is a term used by different theorists in the field of hermeneutics to capture the cognitive and emotional process of distancing ourselves from something we are engaging, such as an idea or situation. It is not disengagement but involves the psychological process of perspective taking, metaphorically stepping back and considering other possibilities or motivations that might be at play in our thinking and feeling. As we move to understanding and interpreting our client's experience, we realize that our thoughts and emotions are not infallible, but we are also aware that we can reflectively step away from the therapeutic experience with our clients and assess the truth that has been achieved in our conclusions and interpretations. In other words, while we are always within a circular hermeneutical method, we are able to prevent a vicious circle by purposefully engaging in reflective processes, preferably in conversation with the client, about the accuracy, veracity, coherence, and authenticity of the therapy. The information we use in this critically reflective place is not just consensus with the client but also the knowledge we have gleaned in our training as psychologists, counselors, and marriage and family therapists. This includes our spiritual/religious knowledge.

It may be tempting at this point to think that this is fine, but it doesn't approach the same level of certitude other domains of knowledge have achieved, such as biology, physics, or chemistry,

Hermeneutics Matter   61

and we would agree. Psychology and its practical application in the form of therapy and counseling is not a natural science and should not aspire to be—it is a human science with its own distinct metrics for truth and certainty that are conceptually distinct from those in the hard sciences. This is not something to be embarrassed or apologetic about but rather should be proudly embraced as a commitment to understanding all the nuances and complexity that human life and relationships entail.

These discussions about the nature of truth and how we form a method of confident judgment are not unique to the field of hermeneutics, and a deeper treatment lies beyond this chapter. We briefly address them here to broaden and anchor our thinking in a method of how we might achieve clinical and theological truth while engaging in clinically integrative practice. Yet, we admit that there is an inherent tension in our clinically integrative work. Even with good-faith efforts and a humble, critical assessment of our practices, there is no perch of reflection that breaks us completely free from our subjectivity. We are not privy to a *God's-eye view*, even when using Scripture.

If we stray too far into the critical domain of reflecting on the truthfulness of our work, we risk succumbing to a decontextualized evaluation of our client, their spirituality, and our role as therapist. This takes us close to power positions that can overestimate what we know and occlude unconscious ways we influence the emergence of integrative moments. Alternatively, we can fall asleep and ignore our responsibility to critically reflect and consider what God might be up to, and again become the unwitting subject of our unconscious agenda. Psychoanalyst and philosopher Donna Orange (1995) captures our thinking here with a concept she refers to as *perspectival realism*. In her thinking, we can acknowledge that subjective understanding is critical in the meaning-making process, but this is not a "turn towards relativism" (p. 4). We all know *in part*, and expanding or deepening our understanding takes conversation as a practical method for attaining a reasonably accurate appreciation of any clinical moment.

SUMMARY AND QUESTIONS FOR CONSIDERATION

In this chapter we have attempted to set the table for an integrative feast. As we consider the topics of tradition, ethics, self-development, and resilience in the remaining chapters, we invite you to sink deeply into your integrative self by embracing a thoughtful consideration of what you bring to the therapeutic relationship. Hopefully we have thoroughly dismantled any notion of the objective and neutral therapist—an ideological myth that still seems to hold sway in many clinical and counseling training programs. We have outlined why this myth is undesirable and indeed impossible for the integrative clinician or anyone involved in clinical work.

The remaining chapters provide an opportunity for you to identify and fill out your hermeneutical frame as you explore the subtle shades of how your experience has shaped and is shaping and refining you into the psychologist, counselor, or therapist God wants you to be. While this may sound like an individual task, it is far from individualistic. We all emerge from and continually engage our families, communities, faith traditions, cultures, and professional guilds as ongoing sources of influence and belonging. Rather than attempting to extract ourselves from these thick, life-giving roots, let's work to develop a welcoming and hospitable attitude to the unique contributions we bring to the healing work of God in the world.

In service of this process, you may want to reflect on the following questions as you move through the rest of this book:

- How has my clinical training fostered or limited the exploration of my faith and spirituality, and what is its influence on how I approach the therapeutic relationship?
- What internal resistances or anxieties do I experience as I consider the uncertainty of clinical work, particularly considering how the therapeutic relationship is a uniquely formed opportunity for the emergence of spiritual work?
- In what ways does framing the clinical relationship as a hermeneutical process create excitement and anticipation when I think about integrating my faith into my work with clients?
- Is there something missing in this chapter that does not quite align with my experience as a beginning or seasoned clinician? In other words, speaking from the uniqueness of your social location (think gender, culture, race, ethnicity, sexuality), did the authors overlook a crucial element of how I have been formed?

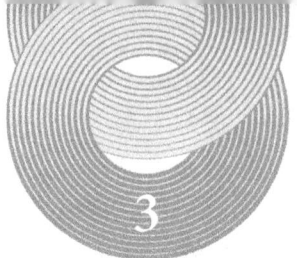

TRADITION MATTERS
THE HERMENEUTICS OF THEOLOGICAL LOCATION

CASE STUDY: Bob, Carol, and Hector

Bob (thirty-five-year-old European American male) had been seeing Carol (thirty-six-year-old European American female) and Hector (thirty-five-year-old Latin American male) in couples' therapy for a few weeks. The couple had been referred to therapy by their pastor, whom Bob once had coffee with when he was marketing his practice. Clearly the pastor thought that Bob was a good guy and potentially a good therapist, so he referred a couple from his own flock.

Bob had done a nice job joining with the couple, identifying their presenting problem, setting the frame, and establishing a treatment contract (e.g., expectations for all involved). The couple seemed engaged and on board with therapy, and the couple noted numerous times that they were so glad that they had found a "Christian therapist." Bob was not exactly sure what the couple meant by a "Christian therapist," or if he did in fact identify as such but had not said any more about it.

The couple identified their presenting problem as "communication issues," fighting numerous times per week (sometimes almost daily) over what seemed like small things. For example, they would fight over how and what to spend money on, they would argue over domestic responsibility and childcare, and, perhaps most damaging relationally, they would fight over frequency of sex, with Hector wanting it more than Carol.

Bob was trained to work from surface to depth, so he began with standard communication-skills training. When that didn't seem to help, he pried a bit deeper and attempted to uncover historical relational patterns in the life of each member of the couple. Psychodynamic practitioners might call these unconscious organizing principles (Stolorow & Atwood, 1992), while more third-wave cognitive-behavioral therapists might call these relational schemas (McMinn & Campbell, 2007). While this helped in small ways, and even though the couple felt what they were doing in therapy was important, something seemed to remain outside everyone's awareness until one particular session.

Bob charged into supervision ready to share this session with his supervisor. The couple had been arguing again about sex. Hector had been frustrated and hurt that they had not had sex for a month and in his frustration began to berate Carol, demanding that she perform her "wifely duty" and have sex with him. Carol, worn out from taking care of most of their domestic life while working full time and doing most of the childcare, had little left to give to Hector at the end of the day. Hector did little to help her feel supported and loved in such a way that sexual intimacy (or any kind of intimacy) would be a natural outgrowth. In their argument, Carol broke down sobbing and confessed that she wasn't sure whether she wanted to have sex with Hector and wasn't sure she was interested in sex at all. This was when Hector pulled his trump card. In exasperation, he pulled out Ephesians 5:22-24, saying that wives were to submit to their husbands because husbands are the head of the house just as Christ is the head of the church. Now Carol felt not only sad, angry, and exhausted but guilty as well. So she indeed did submit, and they had the worst sex ever. Carol submitted but was hurt and angry, and felt demeaned by the experience. Later Hector would comment that he went through with it for the principle but that he knew Carol was resentful, that it didn't feel mutual, and that he too eventually felt angry and sad about it.

WHAT'S GOING ON HERE?

While all couple relationships include conscious and unconscious aspects of power, there were numerous issues going on in this interaction, and subsequently numerous avenues to explore. Bob's supervisor was interested in Bob's response to Hector and asked Bob what he thought about Hector's use of Scripture. Bob said he didn't agree with it. The supervisor asked Bob to clarify. Bob, who had done a fair share of theological reading and some formal training, started explicating exegetical techniques of interpreting Scripture in light of the whole gospel as well as using the historical-critical method, which calls for interpreters to read Scripture in light of the social location in which it was written. In fact, Bob admitted to his supervisor that he found himself quite upset in the session and had begun to overtly challenge Hector's use of Scripture, but this only led to Hector (and Carol!) asking whether Bob really believed in the Bible and whether he really was a Christian. Bob found himself becoming defensive, and the therapeutic alliance with the couple seemed ruptured.

Bob's supervisor invited him to explore his contribution to the rupture, particularly Bob's "theological countertransference." What was central at this point in the treatment was not who had the *true interpretation* (see chapter two) of Scripture but a recognition that Bob and Hector and Carol came from very different theological faith traditions. While they all considered themselves Christians, used similar words such as *Bible*, *Christian*, *Jesus*, *Trinity*, *salvation*, *church*, and even *Christian worldview*, the words they used didn't always mean the same thing. The social location of one's Christian tradition makes a huge difference in how one reads and interprets Scripture, understands theological concepts, and even experiences God. *That is, one's Christian faith tradition is a central aspect of forming one's hermeneutic.*

While the literature on psychotherapy no longer holds to the concept of value-neutral therapy (Richardson et al., 1999), most training programs, even integrative ones, train clinicians as if they can somehow approximate value neutrality. As we hinted at in chapter two, training sometimes sends the not-so-subtle message that therapists should keep their values out of the way and on the back burner. Any countertransference they experience, emanating from their own background and history, should be processed outside therapy, either in supervision or in their own personal therapy. The main problem with this approach (and we will say more about this in chapter four) is that it conceptualizes the therapist's subjectivity as a problem to be managed or sequestered. This may lead to a situation in which the therapist's subjectivity, and hence their contribution, is ignored, which paradoxically makes it more likely to be covertly and even coercively enacted in the therapy, as it was in Bob's getting into a theological argument with Hector and Carol (Dueck & Reimer, 2009).

By ignoring, attempting to bracket, or even disavowing one's subjectivity, the therapist is restricting his capacity to acknowledge it, reflect on it, notice its impact, and even use it in the therapy room. Theorists who write on multicultural competence have been arguing this for some time (Dueck & Reimer, 2009). For example, a Caucasian therapist working with an African American client must attempt to be mindful not only of the racial and cultural issues that might be operating in her client but of the assumptions and blind spots that are operating in her due to her own racial and ethnic location.

WHAT ARE TRADITIONS?

What do we mean by *tradition*? We are using the term in a similar manner to philosophical ethicist Alasdair MacIntyre (1984). For our purposes, a tradition includes a particular religion or sect within that religion (e.g., Christian denomination) but is also much more. Tradition is best understood as a kind of culture. A culture may be conceived of as a particular people group embodying practices, rituals, language (even jokes), and customs that orient the group toward particular morals, values, and norms. By being immersed in a culture, humans *know* things such as what is valuable, what they should strive for, what is ultimate in life; in religious language, we might say what to worship. We italicize the word *know* because it is a kind of implicit or tacit knowledge (Polanyi, 1958), that is, much more than knowing in a conscious, cognitive way.

Tradition is to humans as water is to fish. Fish aren't consciously aware of the water they are swimming in; nevertheless, it greatly affects them. Culture, tradition—human water—shapes and forms human persons, and yet often in psychological circles, the tendency has been to focus only on the conscious elements of culture or religion/tradition. While family systems theory has branched out from a focus solely on the immediate nuclear family to include societal influences, we are suggesting that tradition must include the much more pervasive unconscious, preconscious, or implicit knowledge we bring to our clinical understanding (Polanyi, 1958).

In a sense, what we call tradition may be akin to what has been termed *endogenous psychology* (Dueck & Reimer, 2009). We suggest that endogenous psychology is not just about culture, ethnicity, or social location but must also include the particular locale of our clients' religious traditions. Clinically, cultural psychology is not an add-on discussed only when issues of race or ethnicity differ between therapist and client. The kind of tradition-based integration we are advocating here centralizes the entanglement of culture in all aspects of the therapeutic relationship.[1] But before we elaborate further, it might be important to discuss how we got to a kind of detraditioned therapy.

MacIntyre (1984) says that a goal of the Enlightenment was to use the scientific method to discover universal truth that could be generalized to all people. To accomplish this, science had to strip away anything that sounded like subjectivity, including all aspects of tradition (e.g., culture, ethnicity, religion). But something quite dangerous happened in this project. By stripping away tradition, we lost the particularities of specific people groups. For example, we lost much of the information about how people go about deciding how they should live and how they arrive at an image of the good life. That is, we lost a methodology from which to understand how people go about making rational ethical and moral decisions.

This stripping away is not only descriptive of what happened but became prescriptive. Individuals within society unknowingly began to live into this *traditionless* perspective. MacIntyre (1984) argues that with no tradition, there is nothing in which to ground one's image of the good life or to make ethical and moral decisions, to claim what is ultimate. People were left to fall back on personal preference, or what he terms "emotivism" (p. 11). In simple terms, this is an ethic that most North Americans are familiar with: *If it*

---

[1] See the unnumbered figure in chapter 1 and notice how culture is not a separate integrative matter but in fact permeates all of the 5 domains.

seems right to me, then it is ethical. If we add a bit of humanistic philosophy to the equation, it might expand to *If it feels right to me and isn't hurting anyone else, it is ethical.* Of course, this raises the question, who gets to decide whether it is hurting someone else? Further, who gets to decide that "what seems right" is actually good for me?

MacIntyre (1984) isn't suggesting that the world should be one homogenous tradition in which everyone agrees, but he is arguing that it is impossible to conduct truly rational and meaningful moral discourse when ethical emotivism is the organizing principle. He argues that we can only make cogent ethical statements from within a particular tradition that provides us with an ethical horizon and that we can only have important ethical discourse with other traditions when we can acknowledge the other's and our own. He further asserts that traditions need to and do change from time to time. Change is not the problem; what MacIntyre fears most is that the fallout of the Enlightenment leaves people traditionless, left to construct personal ethical systems from the scraps and poorly formed images of the good life, steeped in the individualism (at least in the West) of the surrounding culture without ever truly reflecting on these ethical scraps.

As Christian clinicians, we worry about this too. Perhaps you are familiar with concepts such as *narrative* and understand the idea that humans are storytelling and story-formed beings. These stories (read: tradition) shape and form us in unconscious ways and are deeply embedded within the various institutional structures (read: water) of which we are a part (read: swim in). We may unconsciously buy into numerous cultural narratives that we are blind to, such as consumerism, individualism, nationalism, or other "isms" that ultimately form our values, morals, norms, and images of the good life. These cultural narratives or traditions even infiltrate our religious traditions, which helps explain how systemic racism and White supremacy became embedded within Christian traditions, while most individual believers claim not to be racist (e.g., Hoard & Bland, 2023). Consequently, we end up not even detecting how some of these narratives or traditions run counter to a religious tradition, or story, that we and our clients claim to hold dear. Our only hope is a kind of distanciation (chapter two) to become aware of how we are being enlisted, conscripted, and formed by the traditions all around us—religious and otherwise. We must become conscious of our Christian faith traditions, our hermeneutic locations, in order not to be blinded by them and not to inadvertently or coercively force them on our clients.

Think back to Bob, Carol, and Hector above. What are the many traditions that are influencing the three of them? There appear to be at least two different Christian traditions at work operating in tandem with traditions related to race, gender, gender power, marital relationships, and how to read Scripture. For example, is it possible that Hector's Latin American cultural heritage has infused his understanding of masculinity and gender (Valdez et al., 2023)? Even if there is conscious rejection of male dominance over woman, how might Hector's particular experience of Latin cultural values regarding gender relationships in marriage be affecting his and Carol's reading of Scripture? Moreover, given Bob's White, educated, upper-middle-class social location, how might his views on gender be influenced by feminist ideas and entangle with a White cultural assumption about egalitarianism in marriage?

We are calling therapists and counselors to mine both their own traditions and those of their clients. As therapists working integratively, it matters that we look deeply not only into both religious and secular traditions that are at work in ourselves and our clients but also the ways in which these traditions might conflict with one another or unconsciously fuse, both between client and therapist as well as within the client's self. Tradition matters.

Mining tradition. What does it mean to mine our own and our clients' traditions? Let's first begin with some definitions and examples of traditions that may influence therapist and client. Keep in mind that traditions are always connected to and pointing toward ethics (i.e., values, morals, norms, and images of the good life).

Religious traditions include but are not limited to the type of world religion one espouses (e.g., Christianity, Judaism), branch of that faith (e.g., Protestant, Catholic), denomination (e.g., Baptist, Presbyterian, nondenominational), and regional and cultural differences found within the same denomination.

Ethnic/race/nationality traditions include common national or geographic demarcations such as African and Filipino, as well as origin of birth and even regional location of upbringing (e.g., south vs. north, west vs. east). While we concur that race is a social construction, we also recognize that it is undoubtedly formative (depending again on the cultural setting in which one was raised and lives), so we subsume it under ethnicity but never want to ignore its powerful, often implicit, impact. This is especially marked for people of color who live and operate as minorities in largely White cultural spaces and must adopt what W. E. B. Du Bois (1903) calls a *double consciousness*. A concept describing the subjective experience of racialized oppression, double consciousness refers to the internal state of *twoness* wherein a person of color is conscious of their own racial identity as well as how this identity is perceived and responded to by a White-majority culture.

Social traditions is a catchall phrase we use to describe what Smith (2009, 2016) calls "cultural liturgies." This is what MacIntyre might call a tradition, psychologists might call a story or narrative, and philosopher Charles Taylor (2003) would call "social imaginary" (p. 23). A liturgy is an often implicit set of practices and rituals, precognitive or unconscious to the participants (think water and fish again), that shapes and forms persons toward a particular set of *ultimate concerns*. This is about ethics, morals, values, norms, and the good life. For example, consider the cultural liturgy of individualism. The rituals here would shape persons to live for oneself, to make decisions in isolation, and to put one's individual rights over the common good of the group, to name just a few. This ethic points one toward an image of the good life where human happiness and ultimacy is a world in which persons are completely and utterly unencumbered from the constraints of others (read: American liberty and the pursuit of happiness). Or imagine the cultural liturgy of consumerism. The rituals and practices here are buying and obtaining, getting yours before someone else does. This breeds not only an internal sense of scarcity in the world but competition (another practice) where the winner takes all. The image of the good life in this story is that ultimacy lies in being able to attain whatever one wants whenever one wants it, and that the good life is obtained by being filled up.

The careful reader may begin to imagine other kinds of traditions that could be operating outside awareness all the while deeply influencing a person. We invite you to engage in just such imaginative work. What all traditions have in common is that (1) they deeply influence persons mostly outside conscious awareness, (2) they define and point persons toward an image of the good life (i.e., what one holds as the ultimate good), (3) a person can internalize more than one tradition that at times may be in conflict with another, and finally (4) even if not overtly recognized as religious, they operate as religious-ethical systems—what Don Browning and Terry Cooper (2004) call "moral philosophies" (p. 23). In other words, again, these traditions operate in the realm of ethics. They describe to and for us what we should value, how we ought to live, and provide practices that point us toward the ultimate goal of life (i.e., the image of the good life).

Traditions develop and are incorporated throughout the lifespan. From our earliest upbringing to the social and political settings we become embedded in, we are influenced and shaped by these traditions. At times we may consciously and deliberatively chose to engage in a tradition (e.g., religious conversion or joining a political party), but at other times we are thrown into settings not of our choosing (e.g., the part of the world we were raised in, our gender, sexual orientation, race, ethnicity, etc.). Both chosen and unchosen, traditions (and here we are especially focusing on our Christian faith traditions) form the conscious and unconscious coloring of our hermeneutical lenses as we discussed in chapter two.

It is also important to note that traditions can operate for good and/or ill. As we alluded to above, traditions are not value neutral; they shape our expectations for how life should be. For example, this is why, for White individuals, White normativity is often not even detected. However, we would argue that traditions that oppress others through mechanisms such as sexism or racism are wrong, whereas traditions that shape love of neighbor and care for the common good are good. Yet, even that last sentence is steeped in a particular tradition. To reiterate, most of our traditions are internalized in such a way that we don't reflect on them; they are operating outside awareness, and yet their impact is profound. We may not know why we believe (i.e., feel) something to be true, but it just feels right and therefore must be right, and we can't understand why others don't see it our way. All the while it is an unacknowledged tradition working its influence.

Of course, we recognize that we are not saying something entirely new. We are reiterating what philosophers, psychologists, anthropologists, and others have known for a long time. But we hope that you are getting an understanding of why it is so important for therapists to mine their traditions and the traditions of their clients. Let us just summarize for the sake of clarity. We must mine our own and our client's traditions because:

First, traditions are often unconscious (i.e., outside our awareness) and therefore unknown sources of our motivations, ethics, morals, norms, and values. They offer and point us toward an image of the good life—something we may silently be striving for while unaware of it. They shape not only what we see but what we expect to see.

Second, if we have become disconnected from tradition or believe we can be traditionless, we will fall back into either unacknowledged traditions (e.g., stories) that affect us in unsuspecting ways, or even into what MacIntyre (1984) calls emotivism (if it feels good to me, it is ethical).

Third, humans can hold conflicting traditions, which may in fact be the source of their difficulties. For example, a person may claim to espouse a Judeo-Christian ethic of the golden rule or loving one's neighbor while at the same time engaging in life in ways that pathologizes or even dehumanizes those who are different. Some Christians have participated in practices that oppress certain people groups, or they spend most of their time acquiring wealth to the neglect of their family. Many times, these situations involve an insidious syncretism (a blending of Christianity and certain sociocultural values), which frequently results in a self-serving distortion of faith priorities. Think of the case that opened this chapter. As discussed earlier, it may be that Hector is operating within a series of conflicting traditions. He claims to aspire to the Christian ethic to love his neighbor as himself, but he repeatedly expects and even requires his wife to subjugate herself to his needs and demands. This not only hurts his wife but hurts Hector as he lives from an internally conflicted state, which may lead to confusion and shame.

Finally, when engaging in therapy or counseling, the traditions of both therapist and client are operating in the background *and* foreground. Not knowing how and when these are operative may lead to serious miscommunication, misunderstandings, and even coercion in the therapeutic dialogue.

Family resemblances and confusions of tongues. We have found the linguistic philosophy of Ludwig Wittgenstein (2009) particularly helpful in regard to misunderstandings in dialogue. Space doesn't permit a deep exploration of Wittgenstein's philosophical import for psychotherapy and counseling. In short, he argued that words don't have inherent meaning but only mean something given the context in which they are used. For example, take the simple word *game*. A baseball game is quite different from a board game, although there are obviously similarities. But what if someone is "running a game" on you, or a love interest is "playing games" with your heart? The meaning of the word *game* changes dramatically given the context in which it is used.

As we mentioned above, traditions are like cultures in that they contain morals, values, norms, rituals, practices, an implicit image of the good life, ethics, and even language. While various traditions may share some common language, idioms and vernacular will be unique; the words they use have particular meaning, which coincides with that specific tradition. To use a religious example, think of the term "the *sovereignty* of God." Many different Christian traditions use this term, but they may mean wildly different things. Whereas a Calvinist may use this phrase to mean that God is the author and creator of all things, including our day-to-day experiences and happenings, a Wesleyan may use the same phrase to suggest that God's ultimate will shall be done but that humans retain individual freedom in their daily choices.[2]

Traditions give meaning to our language; therefore, it is essential that therapists and counselors mine their own and their client's traditions because if they don't, they may engage in what Wittgenstein (2009) terms a mistake of "family resemblance" (p. 67). This is when people use the same word but mean vastly different things. A client and therapist might speak of the sovereignty of God but are actually speaking past each other in profound ways. This is what we call a confusion of tongues.

Mining the therapist's traditions. Many graduate programs in clinical or counseling training require a minimum number of hours for their students to attend therapy/counseling, but unfortunately many don't. Yet, even if it is required, this says nothing about its usefulness. Are these students in therapy with master clinicians who have experience treating therapists in training? Do the students enter therapy as a requirement to be accomplished (i.e., to check off the hours needed), or do they enter to truly understand themselves in ways that can positively affect their work? We believe that good therapy for therapists in training helps the student develop experience and empathy for clients by being in the role of client, but also begins the lifelong process of uncovering unconscious blind spots, hermeneutics, and traditions that will influence the student's own therapy work.

So, our first suggestion for how therapists can mine their own traditions is to get into meaningful therapy. Find a therapist who has experience working with therapists. In therapy, talk about

---

[2]We recognize there are many individual differences within these broad theological categories of Calvinist and Wesleyan.

yourself, but also talk about your clinical work. Of course, you will talk about your clinical work in supervision, but you are limited there in how deep you can go into your own countertransference reactions. In fact, a good supervisor should send you to your therapist when the supervisor detects that there is something deeper and more personal going on that is affecting the therapy. A rule of thumb is that a supervisor may raise countertransference issues but should not delve into them. Remember, you can talk about your clinical work in therapy in confidential ways—and your therapy is also confidential. It's a win-win.

There are additional ways to mine our traditions, but remember this is a lifelong process. Even good therapy doesn't illuminate or erase all our blind spots. Traditions *provide the hermeneutical structures for how we engage the world*. The goal isn't to eliminate our traditions or our hermeneutical way of engaging the world but to become more and more aware. Good therapy is like dropping a pebble in a pond. We hope that good therapy will stir ripples in us (and our clients), enabling us to ponder in new and different ways for years to come. By gaining awareness of our various traditions, we don't strive for value neutrality but awareness of how, when, and to what extent our traditions are interacting with the traditions of our clients. This allows us to use our own and our clients' subjectivity as part of the therapeutic process. We can make these traditions talkable in ways that advance the work.

Here are a few ways outside therapy that you can mine your own traditions.

First, explore your theological faith tradition—you have one! You can do this by asking yourself a series of questions and engaging in a few exercises.

- What faith did you grow up in?

- What were the theological commitments of that faith? If you are a "theological mutt," who has attended several different traditions during your development, try to think through all of them as well as the most formative and even the most recent.
- If you have grown up in nondenominational churches, remember these too are traditions with theologies. Do they have statements of faith? Explore their websites to see whether you can determine their core beliefs. Where was the pastor educated? Talk to your pastor about these things.

Second, choose three topics and ask yourself what your tradition believes about them (e.g., how to read the Bible, gender roles, divine-human interaction [e.g., divine control vs. human freedom]).

Third, try to understand the rituals and practices of your faith tradition.

- Do you understand and can you articulate the image of the good life it espouses? In other words, do you know what issues of ultimacy it points toward? How is one to live one's life? Is faith just to get your ticket to heaven punched, or is it for more?
- Now, explore your own development. Do you still subscribe to these same beliefs and practices? If you don't, how have you changed, what instigated this change, and how do you feel about it?

Fourth, in this book we are focused mostly on faith traditions, but it is essential that in the overall training of clinicians this process is repeated with a number of other traditions, including but not limited to race, ethnicity, socioeconomic status, gender, and sexual orientation. We also recommend taking courses or continuing-education workshops in any of these areas as wonderful ways to promote tradition self-awareness.

Fifth, we believe that good clinicians are lifelong learners. So, in addition to attending courses, you can also read. Too many clinicians make the mistake of reading (if they do read) only writings on technique (usually the newest and latest) or maybe theory but ignore reading in ways that may illuminate their unconscious traditions. For example, Orange (2016) argues for ethical reading, in which clinicians read history, memoir, fiction, and nonfiction regarding other people groups of which they have little knowledge. We have found that reading first-person memoirs of people of color, or theology and sociology written by people of color, has not only greatly deepened our understanding and empathy for these individuals and groups but illuminated our own tradition-based blind spots. The same can be true of first-person accounts of individuals from other faith traditions.

Mining our client's traditions. Clinicians differ widely in their approaches to gathering historical data and conducting intakes in therapy. Some actually send pages and pages of intake questionnaires to potential clients before therapy has even begun. Others have a simple consent form signed before beginning but a structured interview process conducted in the first session or first few sessions. Others use a consent form but let history gathering unfold naturally over time. We encourage you to work in a manner that feels most natural to you and your client and is prescribed by your supervisor. Nevertheless, we also respect those structured interviews that obtain a detailed religious history.

Perhaps because we are both psychoanalytic practitioners, our initial connection with a new client tends to be focused on joining with the client, finding their pain, offering preliminary understanding and realistic hope. We gather information on clients' traditions over time in a more unfolding manner, although we are not opposed to direct questioning. Here are the kinds of things we are thinking and even at times asking directly.

- In what faith tradition did this person grow up?
- Do they continue to subscribe to it?
- How important is this tradition to them?
- What do they hold as most sacred in their lives?
- Do they engage in the rituals and practices of their faith tradition?
- What are the core or central tenets of that faith tradition? For example, how do they understand the role of the Bible or how God operates in their day-to-day life? What does God expect of them?
- How much does their life revolve around faith? How does it affect their daily life, that is, their decisions and actions?
- Are their faith community and the practices of that community resources for them?
- What is their God representation? In other words, what images, feelings, and emotions are evoked when thinking about God and their relationship to God?
- Is there any shame or guilt (or trauma) that is religiously motivated and is negatively affecting the client?
- How are all the above questions related to traditions steeped in ethnicity, race, and culture?
- Does the client want to incorporate their tradition in the work?
- Would it be necessary to bring in persons from the tradition (e.g., pastor) to facilitate the work?
- What psychological purpose might the tradition serve for them?

BOB, CAROL, AND HECTOR

Let's return to the case of Carol and Hector and see whether we might help Bob navigate these traditioned waters. We saw above that Bob's supervisor had already begun to help him see that in the last session he was dealing not only with his own tradition-based countertransference but also with a class of traditions and now, borrowing Wittgenstein (2009), we could say a *family resemblance* problem. Even though all three of the people involved claimed Christianity as their tradition, they didn't know the different ways in which that claim affected them through unconscious practices, rituals, and implicit beliefs.

When Hector began to use Scripture to obtain what he wanted (sex) from Carol, Bob was deeply affected because he had a different way of interpreting Scripture. He didn't know that Carol and Hector were biblical literalists, which meant that they believed that the Bible was to be interpreted through a literal reading. They believed that if the Bible said wives should submit to their husbands, then this meant that the husband was the final decision maker, the one in charge, and what he wanted should happen. And even while this ended up hurting Carol and leaving her resentful, she too was a literalist and so believed that this was her role in the marriage. This ultimately led to their disconnecting intimacy. There may have also been cultural issues at work in all three such as patriarchy. Further, as we stated earlier, Hector may be unconsciously influenced by a cultural tradition of gender, Carol by an evangelical tradition of female complementarity, and Bob by a Caucasian feminist tradition he developed in graduate school.

Of course, as therapists and counselors, we recognize that there is a lot going on here in addition to how each person of the triad interprets Scripture. There are undoubtedly psychological issues regarding intimacy for both in their family of origin. Present problems and conflicts from their histories are being concretized in the sexual relationship, and we may hypothesize that external stressors (children in the home, stress at work, even sociological issues) are also affecting the couple and their intimacy. But, as mentioned above, we clinicians often get mired in the psychological, forgetting that traditions such as religion may also be contributing to the problems.

Bob's supervisor helped Bob explore his own faith tradition, enabling him to understand his highly negative reaction to Hector and even to Carol, who sided with Hector. Bob came to understand how the way he was intervening might feel unsafe to the couple, as it was implicitly and explicitly challenging a core belief they had about the Bible. In doing so, Hector and Carol wondered whether they could trust Bob or whether he was even a fellow believer. Without this understanding, Bob and the couple could become bogged down in what contemporary relational psychoanalysis calls an *enactment* (Benjamin, 2018). This is where the transference/countertransference of both client (in this case a couple) and therapist becomes stuck in what Jessica Benjamin calls a complementary "doer-done-to" interactive stance. Both parties lose perspective and empathy for the other and begin to attempt to force the other to submit to their will. In this case, the couple might push Bob to accept their biblical understanding of gender roles, which would leave Bob feeling "done-to." Conversely, Bob might push the couple to accept his version of biblical gender roles, and the couple would then feel like they were the "done-to." In a kind of back-and-forth, teeter-totter-like interaction of push-and-pull and splitting, both parties become entrenched in their perspective, and the work stalls or stops altogether in premature termination.

To move out of an enactment like this, Benjamin (2018) states that the therapist must find a way to move the therapeutic couple to what she describes as the third or mutual recognition. The third is a place of refocused empathy and a larger perspective of what is going on in the therapeutic space. It is a space where all parties can recognize each other's separate subjectivity with respect and empathy. Sometimes this requires the therapist to actually comment on the enactment/stalemate, but sometimes the therapist's personal recognition of what is going on can enable the therapist to intervene differently and get them back on track.

Bob's supervisor helped him see that he had lost empathy for the couple by not being cognizant of their tradition (and his own), which for so long had provided them with a hermeneutic for how the world worked and how to live in it, and offered them rituals and practices that shaped their ethics, morals, norms, values, and sense of ultimacy. Their particular form of faith had pointed them toward their image of the good life. While Bob believed that their interpretation of biblical gender roles was hurting them as a couple, they couldn't reflect on this because they felt defensive. It was as if Bob were pulling out a cornerstone of their faith/tradition, in this case, how to interpret Scripture. For Carol and Hector, to challenge the way they interpreted Scripture activated an unconscious fear that the whole edifice of their faith would fall apart. In helping Bob understand the enactment between his and his client's' traditions, the supervisor attempted to help Bob find empathy again for the couple in order to get them off the teeter-totter and back into the third of mutual recognition and respect.

As the couple entered therapy for the next session, the tension was palpable. Bob waited a minute or so, as he usually did at the beginning of a session, to see whether the couple would bring up anything, but seeing their silence, he jumped in. He noted that it seemed to him that there had been a break in their connection in the last session, and he thought he might know why. Bob owned that he may have inadvertently reflected a negative view of how both Hector and Carol understood Scripture. He apologized for this and said that he really wanted to understand what Scripture meant to them, how they were taught to read it, and how they used it in their daily lives, even in their marriage. The couple visibly relaxed, and Hector began to share what their church taught about Scripture.

While Hector and Carol both used words they had heard in their church, such as *literal, infallible,* and *inspired,* they were hard-pressed to explain what these words actually meant. As therapists, we have often observed this disconnect between words people adopt from their churches and clear understanding of their meaning. This tends to be true in both progressive and conservative denominations. Bob demonstrated a genuine spirit of curiosity of the couple's view of Scripture and respect for their tradition from which it came. He was able to see and articulate back to the couple how important this tradition was for them, and in doing so the rupture in the relationship began to heal. Mutual recognition and the third were being reestablished.

Over many sessions the couple relaxed, and they were able to begin to see how their view of Scripture, while not *the* central problem in their relationship, at times was being used in ways that were not honoring to either partner. Sometimes both Hector and Carol lived in a kind of conflict between traditions in their faith (e.g., wives submit, consider others better than yourself). At times the couple used Scripture as a way to avoid talking about particular areas of disagreement. It was easier to fight about Scripture (something outside their relationship) than it was to talk about the vulnerability of their feelings. Through respecting their tradition, Bob was able to join with the couple, creating a safe space, which allowed for the exploration of other biblical truths for the couple such as mutual submission and respect and honoring of one another. New opportunities were created for the couple to talk about sex not as something that was one person's right and the other's obligation but as a mutual act of surrender that was honoring and joining when both partners felt respected, loved, and nurtured. This led to conversations about what sort of behaviors, practices, and rituals in their marriage might lead to these important feelings.

Hector and Carol had several other interpersonal issues to explore in the course of therapy. Additional traditions were important therapeutically. Hector's Hispanic culture and the related gender issues needed time on center stage. Carol's White-European culture also needed to be understood in terms of gender, sexuality, and faith. And, of course, Bob also needed to be aware of, own, understand, and possibly even disclose his traditions in all these areas for therapy to continue to progress.

SUMMARY AND QUESTIONS FOR CONSIDERATION

What we have attempted to demonstrate in this chapter, albeit simply, is one of the clinical implications for what we discussed concerning hermeneutics in chapter two. One's faith tradition (like other cultural issues) has a powerful impact on everything from identity to how one understands ethics, morals, and the end goal of human life (i.e., the good life). Therapists and clients from similar faith traditions, for example, Christianity, may use similar words but make hermeneutical mistakes in assuming that they mean the same thing. This may lead to a kind of enactment in which both therapists and client attempt to force their "correct" hermeneutic on the other. Like the conflict between Hector and Carol, this is what Benjamin (2018) might call a complementary doer-done-to enactment. At these moments the clinician has most likely lost her empathic stance. To emerge successfully from this kind of enactment, one must notice what is going on in the clinical relationship, own one's own tradition, and then reengage the client in empathy.

Hopefully this example has demonstrated how important the role of an integrative supervisor, as well as one's own integrative therapist, is to this work. Occasionally a religious student may enter therapy with a great but nonreligious therapist who may not be open to or know how to practice spiritually integrated therapy (Pargament, 2011). In this scenario, the religious student may miss the opportunity to work with their own religious issues and tradition in their personal therapy. For this reason, we offer a number of questions therapists can ask themselves when it comes to thinking about their own traditions.

- What is my religious or spiritual tradition?
- How important is this tradition?
- How involved am I in the tradition?
- How important is my religious community and practices?
- How do I differ from the tradition I was raised in?
- What are some of the central issues in my tradition (e.g., biblical inerrancy, God's sovereignty, God-human relationship, etc.)?
- Are there ways in which my tradition is an important source of my coping and being in the world?
- Are there ways in which my tradition has been a hindrance to my psychological growth?
- What does my tradition suggest is the goal of life?
- What are the interpersonal ethics attached to my tradition?
- Are there other religious or spiritual traditions that my tradition would conflict with?

Other questions may help integrative clinicians understand their own traditions and the ways in which they might affect therapy work. What we have attempted to emphasize is that not knowing the impact of one's own tradition and not acknowledging the client's tradition can lead to countertherapeutic enactments, bringing therapy to a standstill, stalemate, or even premature termination. As mentioned above, sometimes simply becoming aware of the enactment allows the therapist to return to empathy and respond differently, but sometimes, as we saw above with Bob, it might require a kind of disclosure, where the therapist essentially says, "Oops, I'm sorry." We have offered practical ways in which therapists can mine both their own and their client's traditions. In this sense we have taken the idea of hermeneutics from chapter two and grounded it in the clinical moment related to one's religious history. In the next chapter we venture to dig even deeper as we begin to explore how ethics are not only formed from our hermeneutical traditions but permeate even our clinical theories themselves.

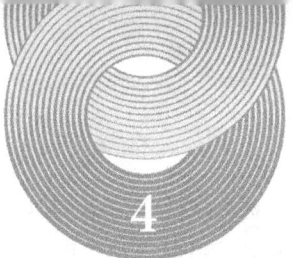

ETHICS MATTER
THE HERMENEUTICS OF ULTIMACY

CASE STUDY: Sheryl and Doi

Doi (thirty-year-old female, Chinese, cisgender, heterosexual, Christian) was in her third session with client Sheryl (fifty-five-year-old female, Caucasian, cisgender, heterosexual). Sheryl had come to therapy complaining about marital problems that seemed to her to be unfixable. She and her husband had been married for over thirty years and had been to see at least two marital therapists to no avail. Their three adult children were grown, out of the house, and fairly independent, although none of them had settled into a long-term romantic relationship.

Sheryl said that she had come to therapy by herself because she needed help figuring out what she wanted to do next. She wasn't sure that she wanted to try anymore to save the marriage but didn't feel settled on divorce either. She recognized that she had a long history of difficulty making decisions. She waffled about marrying her husband, fretted about having children, flitted from job to job, and although she had once tried to leave her husband, she felt too guilty and returned home. She claimed that her husband had an addictive personality and was verbally mean, although never violent (she admitted that she held her own in their fights), and that he conceptualized most of her personal problems as stemming from her anxiety. On the other hand, she wasn't sure that her husband could make it without her, and if he were to fall apart emotionally, due to divorce, she wasn't sure she could live with the guilt.

In the first two sessions, Sheryl revealed a history of being a somewhat sensitive child whose parents had high expectations for her. She reported that her parents were not very emotionally available to her, and she remembered as a child living with a kind of general anxiety, fearing that her decisions would lead to disappointing someone. Over the years she developed a pattern of ruminative thinking, what she called "spinning," which could include obsessively thinking about a decision and/or berating herself for not being able to make one.

During the third session, Sheryl was talking about how she perceived her husband's wants and needs. She articulated what she thought he wanted from her as a wife, what he wanted from the marriage, and what it would be like for him if she were to leave. At this point in her training, Doi had been trained in a broadly eclectic manner, mostly a humanistic style (i.e., client centered), with some training in cognitive-behavioral techniques and a little bit of psychodynamic understanding. For most of the session, Doi simply reflected and empathized with Sheryl. Finally, when there was a break in Sheryl's commentary, Doi empathically said, "It is very clear to me that you know exactly what your husband feels and thinks, but I wonder what you want?" Without hesitation, Sheryl responded, "That's the difference between psychology and religion, isn't it? Psychology is all about the individual, and religion is all about the 'other.'"

WHAT IS GOING ON HERE?

Doi stopped dead in her tracks. She wasn't sure whether this was a rhetorical question, but nevertheless she didn't know what to say next. The client had been referred to her by a friend but not for religious reasons. In fact, in the intake session Sheryl had said that she was vaguely agnostic with some Mormon background on her mother's side. But what really shocked Doi, although she couldn't have articulated it at the time, was that Sheryl was actually presenting an *ethical critique of psychotherapy*. Sheryl was suggesting that, at its core, psychotherapy is about the individual client's priorities and therefore hierarchical, placing the needs of the individual client over any kind of communal, relational, or religious responsibility or ethic to the other.

Doi quickly recognized this as a critique, but she had to admit that she had never thought about it that way before. How could she have missed this? After all, she was an integrative therapist. She wove faith and Christian practice into her work as a psychologist, or at least she tried to. She knew from cultural critiques that Western psychotherapy could be individualistic as opposed to more communal cultures, but she hadn't thought of this in terms of a religious and ethical conflict. Doi believed that Christian faith (which was her background and practice) was deeply anchored in love of neighbor, putting others first, and welcoming the stranger. In fact, these were central to how she thought spiritually about her work as a therapist. But she had naively assumed that armed with her Christian convictions, she could lay these over any psychotherapeutic orientation that she chose and practice without conflict.

At an even deeper level, Doi suffered from what Jeeves and Ludwig (2018) call *concordism*, which they describe as an attempt to harmonize psychology and religion or even to incorporate psychology into Christian theology. Doi's attempt to harmonize the two disciplines had left her blind to a potential conflict between the two. In the blink of an eye, Sheryl had noticed and named the conflict that might have far-reaching implications for their work together and for Doi's work as an integrative therapist.

To make matters even more problematic, Doi recognized that she was also practicing in a way that was antithetical to her own cultural heritage. As a Chinese woman, from a collectivist culture, the group often took precedent over the individual. Doi had unknowingly incorporated not just the ethics of her theoretical orientation but also the Western individualistic ethic underlying it.

THE FOUR STRANDS OF RELATIONAL ETHICS

Ethics matter in our integrative work because they are multidimensional and woven in and through our hermeneutics and traditions. As we discussed in chapter three, traditions are our hermeneutical guides and shape our ethics; they point to an image of the good life, or what ethicists would call a telos. A telos is an end goal. It is what we value as ultimate or what we ultimately value. In theological language, we might say it tells us what we worship—to what we give our hearts (Smith, 2009, 2016). No matter how you look at it, ethics matter. While understanding our traditions can help point us toward these ethics, the ethics themselves can be elusive. In many ways, as we discussed in chapter three, they are hidden in ways that allow us to take them for granted. They can be transmitted to us via the cultural milieu we are steeped in, and they become internalized and forgotten, although still deeply influential. So, while consciously we may be able to articulate a number of values and morals we hold dear, many more ethical issues are implicit in ways of which we are unaware. These become the unacknowledged hermeneutics that shape our lives. Therefore, it is essential that we understand ethics in therapy and counseling, and how we may go about mining them.

Before we can discuss mining our own and our clients' ethics, we first need to flesh out what we mean by *ethics* in psychotherapy.

We subscribe to the four strands of ethics of psychotherapy discussed by Barsness and Strawn (2018), and while they were not originally writing to an integrative audience, we believe their categorization has great import for integration. The four strands are (1) professional ethics, (2) personal ethics, (3) theoretical ethics, and (4) communal ethics. One might ask, why ethical "strands"? The term is used to create a kind of visual image of four strands that, while individually unique, also form a kind of unity. Each is essential, important to the whole, while also maintaining its own unique role. All are important; all must be understood, acknowledged, and even developed. None is strong enough alone to handle the moral discourse of therapy. While strands are woven to create a wholistic ethic at work in both the therapist and the client (in both conscious and unconscious ways), we can actually mine each individual strand to increase our integrative mindset.

First strand: Professional ethics. When clinicians speak about ethics, the first things that usually come to mind are the *professional* ethics of the guild or licensing organization in which the psychologist or counselor is credentialed. These ethics are important and ostensibly are there for the protection of both clients and therapists. They usually include both *dos* and *don'ts*. They are time tested, created, endorsed, and even policed by licensing boards. When these professional ethics are first learned, some new clinicians often comment that they feel tremendous fear of making a mistake, being taken to court, and losing their license. Subsequently, new clinicians may feel frozen, becoming almost robotic in their clinical style, afraid to even practice warmth toward a client for fear of committing an ethical violation.

Professional ethics are needed and important, and should be internalized by new therapists. But the way we will use the concept of ethics in this chapter is deeper and inevitably more complex. We want clinicians to learn and practice in accordance with the ethical stance of their professional guilds. In addition, we also want to call all clinicians, and especially integrative clinicians, to recognize that there are different but equally powerful ethics at work in the practice of therapy and counseling. These ethics have great import when it comes to integration.

Second strand: Personal ethics. Personal ethics are the values and morals we learned at our parents' knees as well as from our communities (faith and otherwise), our cultures, and the zeitgeist of the time. These are usually deeply ingrained, implicit, and partially unconscious. Philosophers refer to this type of hermeneutic phenomenology in a number of ways: horizons of meaning, preunderstandings or pre-prejudice, and so on (Gadamer, 1975; Taylor, 2011). We could even go so far as to refer to this strand as our *personal ethical hermeneutic*. Because the transmission of this strand is so developmental and surreptitious, people are often unable to articulate why they find something to be ethical or unethical. They just *feel it*. Persons see the world through their ethical lens, and it feels like capital-T *Truth* to them. It can be very hard to become aware that this feeling is actually their perspective and not some kind of plumb line, and because it is hard to become aware of it, these internal feelings take the form of convictions that can be very difficult to change.

Ironically, this is one way to understand the therapeutic task of therapy. Clients come to therapy for several reasons and causes, but at the end of the day, one of the most significant actions that psychotherapy and counseling accomplishes is helping clients develop a theory of mind (Fonagy et al., 2004). *Theory of mind* is a philosophical term that refers to a developmental capacity that persons can more or less develop throughout the lifespan. Psychotherapy theorists have used different terms to describe this capacity:

observing ego, mentalizing, intersubjectivity, thirdness (e.g., Benjamin, 2018; Brenner, 1974; Stern, 1985; Stolorow, 2013). This capacity permits for both self- and other reflection, but it is a particular kind of reflection, reflection on a person's internal experience usually intuited through embodied behaviors. In the language of chapter two, theory of mind is the capacity to reflect on one's own hermeneutical lens as well as the lens of others. Having a theory of mind allows one to mentalize; it is the ability to infer the "mental states of other persons based on their behavior, using memories of one's own experiences" (Brown & Strawn, 2012, p. 57). In normal development, this is what allows children to recognize that sometimes they share similar feelings, thoughts, and perspectives with others, but sometimes they don't.

Clients often come to therapy with a diminished theory of mind. They are certain that the way they see the world (i.e., their hermeneutic, fashioned by all their influencing traditions) is the way the world is, and yet this is the very thing that gets them into trouble. We contend that helping clients recognize that this is their *perspective*, and not the "whole truth and nothing but the truth," is in fact the development of a theory of mind. In some way all psychotherapy orientations attempt to do this. They may use different language and emphasize different ways to go about it, and/or emphasize different ways in which perspectives are formed (e.g., affect vs. cognition), but in the end all therapies or counseling models try to help clients understand the way they automatically see the world (i.e., through their hermeneutical traditions) and recognize that others see it differently. Just as our perceptions are automatic, so are most of our behaviors. To develop a theory of mind is to develop an awareness, which in turn creates a growing level of freedom to behave differently in the world.

In the language of this chapter, we could say that in part therapy helps clients recognize their personal ethics. By this we mean helping clients to consciously articulate unconscious commitments to what they value as ultimate or what they ultimately value. Clients often don't understand that what they ultimately value drives their feelings, thoughts, and behaviors. They also don't understand how these unconscious commitments may create conflicts in their lives with others and even with the larger culture in which they find themselves.

To return to our vignette, Sheryl was expressing her understanding that within at least some religious traditions, the value of the other over the self is an explicit ethic. When Doi asked a seemingly innocent question about what Sheryl wanted from the marriage, Sheryl heard an implicit ethic of self first, others second. So, we can see why it *matters* that the integrative clinician mine both their client's personal ethical strand as well as their own. But Sheryl was pointing out something even more interesting. She didn't say that Doi's personal ethic was self over the other but that psychology's ethic was self over the other. This leads us to the next strand.

Third strand: Theoretical ethics. We depart a bit from the original conceptualization of the four strands as conceived by Barsness and Strawn (2018) only in terms of groupings while still maintaining the content. Originally this theoretical strand was conceptualized as consisting of the ethics that a psychotherapy or theory purported counselors *ought to* do.[1] For example, Barsness and Strawn argued that Sigmund Freud postulated a theoretical ethic of *certainty*. Freud believed that the journey to health was to make the unconscious conscious and that he knew, based on his theory, what needed to be revealed. Therefore, it was his job, his

---

[1] Words and phrases such as *ought* and *should* are one of the first signs that ethics are operating, even if in the background.

ethical responsibility, to interpret—that is, to know for the client—to make the unconscious conscious. Anything less or more would be unethical. Barsness and Strawn argue that this theoretical ethic strand can be mined in other theories as well.

> Cognitive Behavioral Treatment models, which originally were seen as the great challengers to psychoanalysis, ironically share an ethic similar to Freud's, in that CBT also tends toward the prescriptive and is dependent upon the certitude of the model. It is the certainty of these two models that directs the therapist's ethical actions. We contend, therefore, that all therapeutic models have implicit ethics based on their theory. (p. 223)

In fact, many theories of counseling and therapy have an implicit theory of certainty, or perhaps it is more accurate to say that they are often taught like that. The therapist/counselor is supposed to know what is going on and what needs to be done, and it is the job of the client, couple, or family to submit to the therapeutic interventions. This puts the therapist in the role of expert and authority while placing the client in the role of passive recipient. This way of conceptualizing therapy and counseling can create anxiety in new clinicians, who feel immense pressure to know exactly what is going in any given therapy at any given time. We would argue that one can detect remnants of this kind of thinking implicitly in most, if not all, contemporary theories of therapy/counseling.

You may already be thinking ahead and recognizing that these ethics of certainty are another brand of hermeneutics, but this time embedded in the therapeutic theory itself. But what happens when the ethics of the theory don't fit a client due to gender, sexual orientation, cultural, racial, or any other number of intersectional differences? Conflict or tension between the therapist and client will be the inevitable result. Our experiences tell us that when a conflict of ethics is not explored, either clients will submit to the authority of the therapist with all sorts of concurrent problems (e.g., colonialism), clients will quietly resist the therapy, or clients will simply drop out (which may have something to do with the high dropout rates of therapy with persons of color).

We need to spend more time on this ethical strand because it's not just that a model or theory of therapy or counseling contains an ethic of what the therapist ought to do but that the theory itself contains an ethical system of health and disorder, what the client should and shouldn't do, and even an image of the good life. This is the language of ethics and hence why ethics matter.

Writers such as Philip Cushman (1995) and Frank Richardson et al. (1999) point out that psychotherapy theories, just like individuals, are products of the times and contexts in which they were developed. Psychotherapy theories can't help but reflect both the individual psychologies of the originators and the zeitgeist of when they lived (Atwood & Stolorow, 1993). Psychotherapy theories are like autobiographies of the individuals who developed them. Browning and Cooper (2004), Christian ethicists and pastoral psychologists, worry that when psychotherapeutic theory is presented as objective, value neutral, and free from ethical concerns, clinicians become "unwitting conspirators with and reinforcements of the dominant social and cultural ethos of our age, i.e., the rational-choice processes of the market and the individualistic and consumerist ethic that it encourages" (p. 25).

Browning and Cooper (2004) argue and demonstrate that schools of therapy and counseling are "practical moral philosophies" or cultures: "But it is my argument that most of the prominent modern psychologies, in addition to whatever scientific value that they may have, do indeed cross over into what must be recognized as types of positive cultures—cultures, indeed, that possess religio-ethical dimensions" (p. 4). Numerous critics of psychotherapy, both within and outside the psychotherapeutic community, have critiqued Western models of therapy as being highly individualistic (Comas-Diaz & Rivera, 2020; Dueck & Riemer, 2009). In ethical terms, this means that the individual is the sole source of truth, ethical reflection, and decision making. Ethics become a matter of personal preference: what feels good or right to me is ethical. Remember that in the previous chapter on tradition, we discussed this tendency, considering what moral philosopher Alasdair MacIntyre (1984) calls emotivism.

So, even if she didn't necessarily believe it, when Doi asked her question to Sheryl about "what she wanted," Sheryl heard the implicit ethical echo of individualism and personal rights. Behind this innocent question is a complex web of ethical philosophical assumptions basically implying that what your culture, community, context, faith, or significant other wants, needs, or deserves is irrelevant, or at the very least can be considered only after you have a thorough understanding of what you, the individual, want. It is an ethical imperative that you take care of yourself and prioritize your persona/individual rights. In her critique, Sheryl was juxtaposing the ethical system she intuited in therapy with one that she understood of religion, in which neighbor love took precedent over self-love.

We are arguing, alongside a great cloud of witnesses, that while psychotherapy and counseling theories present themselves as value free, neutral, and so on, they in fact contain implicit ethical systems or serve as practical moral cultures. However, that is not necessarily the problem. The problem is that "they are thin ethics because they have become decontextualized from any explicit cultural or communal narratives often found within traditional religious, spiritual, and moral systems, leaving them in the realm of ethical emotivism" (Barsness & Strawn, 2018, p. 231). Therefore, the focus of any psychotherapy or counseling devolves to technique and effectiveness, while the goal becomes the transformation of the client-consumer into a well-adjusted member of society (Fromm, 1950; Wright et al., 2014).

It doesn't take an advanced degree in cultural psychology to see how problematic this can be when working with clients from non-Western cultures, with clients of color, or with sexual or gender minorities. Practicing therapy or counseling while unthinkingly using a Western theory, which ignores tradition and has the ethics inextricably embedded in the theory itself, is to engage in a practice that might in fact do violence to clients who don't come from that perspective (Dueck & Reimer, 2009). While the language of violence might be off-putting in such a time as ours, when violent political rhetoric has become the norm and physical violence of women and persons of color is rampant and minimized, we believe it is an important word to retain. While never wanting to minimize the very real and horrific physical violence happening in this country and around the world, we also believe that therapy, the cure of the soul, is a powerful instrument and if used erroneously may do serious damage to clients' sense of self, heritage, traditions, families, cultures, and religious commitments. To conduct therapy, or enter it as a client, is not for the faint of heart.

We worry that the current ethos in the science of psychotherapy, and its emphasis on effectiveness and empirical validation, avoids asking larger ethical questions that are related to the common good. What is therapy for? What is the end result? Does therapy help individuals cope better in a sick family/society/era? Does therapy ignore the larger issues of poverty, crime, racism, sexism, classism, and all other manner of *isms*, and social justice in general? What should motivate a therapist? Or another way to say this is, *Why should one engage in therapy?* More specifically for this book, *Why should a Christian engage in the practice of psychotherapy?*

If it is true that our clients enter therapy with traditions (as discussed in chapter three) that form within them implicit ethics (e.g., theories of right and wrong, what one ought to do, how one should live, what is health and what is dysfunction, an image of the good life, etc.), and if therapists and their theories also have implicit ethics, then it is not hard to imagine, as Cushman (1995) suggests, that therapy is a *moral discourse*. In other words, a client comes to therapy not just with a psychological problem but at a deeper level with an ethical problem. Life for them is not working like it should; this is ethics. The therapist then engages the client in a conversation (which of course includes the therapist's professional, personal, and theoretical ethics—informed in part by their chosen theory) ostensibly to help the client get their life—their *should*—back in order.

We propose that psychotherapy, even an integrative one, that is ethically thin (i.e., doesn't know how ethics *matter*) may not recognize their client's deeply held ethics, nor acknowledge the ethics with which they approach the counseling relationship. Rather than understanding therapy as a dialogical encounter between two people dealing with ethical questions, the therapist (and unknowingly the client as well) may operate from the position that it is the therapist, not the client, who knows best. It's the therapist, armed with her theory, who really knows what is going on regarding health and how to get there. But we are saying ethics matter because in reality, therapy consists of two persons—client (armed with their personal ethics) and the therapist (armed with their professional, personal, and theoretical ethics)—in a moral conversation about how the client should live. Most graduate training programs don't teach this conceptualization of therapy. We argue passionately that it is essential, maybe especially for the clinical integrative practitioner.

This may be hard to conceptualize in the abstract, so imagine a very short and overly simplistic therapeutic scenario. A client comes in complaining about overbearing work and life stress, not connecting with their spouse and children, and starting to feel a lot of anxiety. It could be argued that this client has bought into a cultural ethic that one "should have it all" and that "the one with the most toys in the end wins." You as the clinician might think that these are unrealistic expectations and that, informed by your theory, real contentment doesn't come with financial acquisitions but through relationships. So, you find yourself beginning to help the client examine what is most important to them by focusing on their relationships. You are in fact bringing an ethical presupposition into the therapy. But what if your client doesn't buy into that ethical stance? What if what they want from you is stress-management and mindfulness practices so they can better cope with the stress they experience while they remain committed to their hectic pace? Though there is no such thing as a value-neutral therapist, we still act as if our theories are value neutral, and we think that if we take a client-centered approach, we can keep our values out of the therapy. It's just not true.

What's a therapist to do? Well, we could try harder to create value-free therapies or value-free therapists. We could take the position that many therapists (and insurance companies) take, overtly or covertly, that being a functional member of society is a "good-enough" outcome of therapy while ignoring the moral and social ills around them. Or perhaps we could become biblical counselors, leaning in hard to a particular way of doing therapy, unapologetically Christian (probably a one-size-fits-all Christianity), believing we know the truth and believing that if clients simply accept it, it will set them free.

We want to suggest a third way. We can't throw off our traditions, and we don't even think that should be a goal. Neither can we escape their accompanying ethics or the implicit ethics embedded within our theories. But we can become aware of them and the hermeneutics through which we view the world (at least to some degree—see distanciation in chapter two). If we can become aware of our traditions, our ethics, and our hermeneutical lens—and how they are operative in our work—then we can avoid covertly forcing them on our clients and create more space for our clients to know and acknowledge theirs.

Acknowledging our own personal ethical strands will force us to answer one of those larger questions we named above: *Why should I practice therapy or counseling?* Becoming aware of the first three ethical strands will help us not only understand therapy and counseling as an ethical discourse but, at times, allow therapists/counselors to serve as moral consultants (Doherty, 1995). We will have more to say about this below.

Fourth strand: Communal ethics. This brings us to the last of the four strands, the communal. We have argued alongside others that while psychotherapy theories can be understood as ethical cultures, practical moral philosophies, or religio-ethical systems, they are thin ethics because they are decontextualized from any particular cultural or communal narrative. In fact, most therapies fall prey to being loosely connected to whatever moral and ethical ethos was current during the time of its inception.

To avoid this dilemma, we advocate that therapists carefully and thoroughly *mine* the first three of their ethical strands and then *develop* a fourth communal ethic, which "must explicitly contextualize itself in thick ethical traditions (philosophically and spiritually) that embrace culture, and communal narratives that are particular, historical, resist reductionism, and embrace specificity, complexity, humility, and human dignity" (Barsness & Strawn, 2018, p. 233). What does this look like? Well, it depends on the integrative therapist. This too can't be formulaic, but it does bring us back to one of those big questions, *Why do we do what we do?*

We (Strawn and Bland) ground our ethical stance in the philosophical/religious tradition of Christianity and even more specifically the life and teachings of Jesus Christ as understood via the Wesleyan-Arminian branch of Protestantism. This communal ethic could be a book in itself, but let it suffice at this point to say a few things about what this means.

We understand all of creation as currently suffering the consequences of brokenness and sin in the world. Nevertheless, redemption and reconciliation are possible through the life, death, and resurrection of Jesus Christ. Persons are invited into discipleship by following Christ's teachings as found in the entirety of Holy Scripture (i.e., Old and New Testaments), particularly the Gospels, and especially the Sermon on the Mount. The goal of the Christian life is not simply or even primarily to be saved and get one's ticket to heaven punched but to participate with Christ through the Spirit in his ongoing eschatological work of making all things new in the here and now, the *already and not-yet* kingdom, on earth as it is in heaven. This eschatological work is to help restore creation to its original order.

This happens whenever the broken are healed, the oppressed are liberated, the needy are served, the loveless are loved, and there is justice for all. This is our *why* of therapy. It is what we think we are doing, and it is why we do it. Whenever we help a person move *even a little bit closer* to what God originally intended for their lives, we are doing God's work and are involved in integration. Sometimes these are incremental moves (moving from severe to moderate depression), and sometimes they are huge (a restored marriage or family).

We could say many other things about our communal ethic contextualized in this particular understanding of Christian faith. For example, we believe that central to this ethic is the centrality of love of God, love of neighbor, and love of self. We believe in modeling one's life after the life, death, and resurrection of Christ. This may mean modeling ourselves after him even in our therapeutic activity of incarnation, crucifixion, and resurrection.[2] It also means casting an exegetical eye toward the surrounding culture (even the culture of psychotherapy) and discerning in what ways there are constructive and destructive exchanges with the narrative of the kingdom of God. For example, is *social adjustment* a goodenough outcome for an integrative therapist if the surrounding society is sick? If our theological position is that human thriving happens via relationality, is it okay to use psychotherapy theories that promote individualism and are based in a capitalistic, consumeristic mindset? Is psychotherapy that consists of a client interacting with a computer-generated algorithm good enough? If welcoming the stranger and foreigner is a theological imperative (another form of neighbor love), is it okay to use theories and techniques developed in a Western context on clients from diverse settings? These are just a few of the things that may come to mind when one develops and owns a communal ethic.

Let us pause and again make clear what we are *not* saying. We are not saying that the goal of becoming aware of the first three strands of ethics and developing a fourth is to force these ethics on to one's clients. Instead, we instruct our students that their hermeneutics, traditions, and ethics must be large and open enough to welcome the other, or no true integration can happen. Paradoxically, the way to avoid covertly coercing our clients into our worldview is by helping clinicians own their own social location. This allows clinicians, often with the help of supervisors, further learning, consultation, and

---

[2]See Hoffman (2011) for a deeply theological understanding of an integrative approach to psychoanalytic psychotherapy. We highly recommend this work to you.

feedback from their clients, to see their blind spots and create space for their clients.

But neither are we implying that the goal is to simply be aware of and bracket our social location. Because psychotherapy is a moral discourse, we believe that issues of ethics and morals will always permeate the therapeutic dialogue. As we noted above, issues of *ought* and *should*, and images of the good life, underlie much of how the client and therapist understand the problem and the solution. There will be times in therapy when the problem that has brought the person to therapy, or at least some part of it, is not psychological as we commonly understand it but ethical. At these times, the therapist may, carefully protecting client autonomy, serve as a kind of moral consultant (Doherty, 1995).

Through the moral discourse of therapy, the dialogue, both therapist and client explore their ethical strands in such a way that it becomes possible to adjust them, even change them in ways that bring greater congruence in the client's life (and maybe the therapist). Moral conflict between the therapist and client doesn't mean simply focusing on what the client wants or simply allowing them to be functional members of society. Good therapy doesn't simply accept or acknowledge one's implicit ethics (wherever they originate) but illuminates them in the service of the client. This awareness allows the client to make decisions regarding how their ethical commitments function in their life and may subsequently lead to their discernment (often done within and as part of a community) of what they desire to hold on to and let go of.

MINING OUR ETHICS

We want to end this chapter by suggesting some ways for therapists to mine both the meaning and impact of their own ethical strands and the ethics of their clients. In the mode of supervision, once again, we offer these suggestions in the form of questions.

Therapist's strand one: Professional
1. What are the ethics of your professional guild?
2. What does it mean for you to practice within those?
3. In what ways might the professional guild's ethics and your own personal, theoretical, or communal ethics conflict?

Therapist's strand two: Personal
1. What kind of morals and ethics did you learn growing up?
2. What do you value as ultimate or ultimately value?
3. Where do you spend your money, your time?

Therapist's strand three: Theoretical
1. What does your theory hold out as health and pathology?
2. What does your theory hold out as the good life?
3. Is your theory more aimed at individualism or communalism?
4. Is your theory large enough and flexible enough to respect the traditions and ethics of clients from diverse cultures and perspectives?

Therapist's strand four: Communal
1. In what philosophical/spiritual/religious context will you anchor your work?
2. What are the ethical commitments of that perspective? What does it see as ultimate value?
3. Is the perspective open and flexible enough to respect clients from different cultures and perspectives?

MINING OUR CLIENTS' ETHICS

Mining our clients' ethical strands will be similar to and different from mining our own. First, clients are not beholden to any professional ethical board of conduct during their treatment. Second, while they may or may not have a consciously articulated theory from which they are living, they are undoubtedly a part of ethical traditions. For this reason, we usually link strands two and three together for clients. Clients do have personal ethics, and some of these may be grounded in a communal ethic, that is, a deep philosophical/spiritual/religious context, even if unacknowledged.

Client's strand two and three: Personal and theoretical (traditions)

1. What do our clients value above all else?
2. Where are they spending their time and money?
3. What can we understand about their ethics/values from their presenting complaint?
4. Where do these ethical commitments come from?
5. Are they experiencing conflicts between different ethical commitments?

Client's strand four: Communal

1. Does the client tend to draw their ethics from a religious perspective? If so, what do you know about it?
2. What are the ethical commitments of that perspective? What does it see as ultimate value?
3. What does this perspective tell them is the goal of life?
4. Are they open to exploring a new ethic?

CONCLUSION

So, where does this leave Doi and Sheryl? What might Doi say to Sheryl's comment? Where can they go next?

We don't see this moment as a problem or mistake but rather an opportunity. By naming the conflict she intuited between psychology and religion, Sheryl let Doi in on something that may or may not be an important part of her unconscious ethical system. And Sheryl's ethical stance may deeply influence her decisions. We would encourage Doi to explore Sheryl's comment. Is Sheryl's decision to end the marriage related in some way to her own character, ethical stance, religious beliefs? Does therapy need to create space for Sheryl to explore an unconscious ethic (i.e., put others first) with other possible equally spiritual ethics (e.g., would it be more ethical to end the marriage because to stay together is doing irreparable damage to them both)? Does Sheryl fear therapy will undermine her personal convictions? Many more areas of exploration can be pursued.

Furthermore, this is an opportunity for Doi. With the help of her client, Doi has now faced an ethical conflict, or at least a conundrum between her own personal ethics and the ethic that seems to be covertly embedded in her chosen theory, not to mention the conflict between the theory's ethic and Sheryl's. Can Doi continue to operate with this theory? How must she retradition it if she does? Is there really a theological conflict here between self-care and other care, or is it more of a nuance that needs to be carefully articulated? And how would Doi feel if Sheryl decided to stay in her marriage because she felt it was the "right thing to do," even if it wasn't what Doi and her theory prescribed as the healthiest thing to do?

We hope you can see that ethics matter and that they build on hermeneutics and tradition in a kind of entwined reciprocity. What is essential is that therapists' mindfulness of these matters enables them not only to see integrative moments when they emerge but also to work with them in life-giving ways.

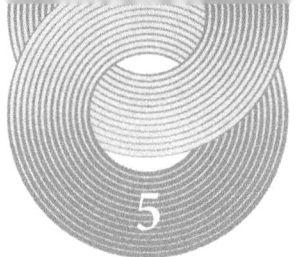

SELF-DEVELOPMENT MATTERS
THE HERMENEUTICS OF FORMATION

CASE STUDY: Isaiah and Dr. Gonzales

The presentation of Isaiah's case was, he thought, routine. As part of the Tuesday morning supervision group, Isaiah, in his final year of counselor training at a well-respected Christian graduate program, was feeling buoyant about his clinical presence and the work he was doing. For the most part his clients were making progress, and his site supervisor was pleased with his contribution to the local nonprofit counseling center that served a local urban community.

Isaiah was interested in couples work and so jumped at the chance to do premarital work with Becca and Andreas. He was looking forward to working with a couple who were excited about marriage rather than the couples he was mostly saddled with—couples perpetually wondering why they had even gotten married. Isaiah was a fan of marriage; he and his wife of fifteen years had two children, and he found great satisfaction in his relationship. He and his wife had met just after graduating from college, and he considered her his best friend.

Other members of the group filed in as Isaiah cued up his video presentation. He wanted to talk about the experience of doing premarital work. He felt good about how he was progressing with his case. Session four, the one he was presenting, was a bit challenging, however, as Becca and Andreas were debating about how to deal with family pressure regarding the wedding guest list. As the conversation intensified, Isaiah had noticed himself favoring Andreas's perspective. Thinking it might have something to do with them both being male, he was looking forward to teasing out any dynamics that may be tilting him from his preferred stance of bidirectional partiality.

The supervision group included Isaiah's faculty supervisor, Dr. Gonzales, and two other student colleagues, Amy and Sydney. At thirty-five years old, Dr. Gonzales, originally from Mexico, was in her third year of teaching graduate school. She had immigrated to the United States from Guadalajara with her family when she was two years old. Amy was African American, and Sydney was White; both were in their mid-twenties. Isaiah was White as well; he was thirty-eight years old. As the video played, it soon became apparent that tension was building between Becca and Andreas. Andreas was becoming more insistent about the importance of inviting his extended family from Europe. Becca was getting angry—why should his relatives, whom he barely knew, have priority over her own cousins, with whom she grew up and who lived very close? It didn't seem fair.

As the conversation continued, Becca brought up that she was doing several things to make this marriage possible, including going to weekly lessons at the local Islamic center. Looking at Andreas, she said, "Is it so hard for you to give a little on your end?" Isaiah had not known about this and asked her to elaborate a bit so he could get the context. Becca explained that for them to get married, Andreas and his family were insisting that they be married in the Islamic tradition. This meant she had to convert.

"I mean, it's fine, my mom was a bit upset, but I didn't even tell my dad. He wouldn't understand," she said. Becca's parents had divorced when she was seven, and she lived most of her life shuffling back and forth.

"I see," said Isaiah. "It feels a bit unfair that you are converting, moving his way, and why can't Andreas give a little on his end, especially about your family?"

"Yeah," responded Becca, "I mean I'm giving up my whole religion," she said, laughing awkwardly, "so the least he could give is to let my family come to the wedding."

Andreas didn't object directly. "I know, but it's my mom. She keeps asking why you have so many cousins who want to come."

"We're Catholic!" retorted Becca. Everyone laughed, including Isaiah.

"How are you feeling about converting?" asked Isaiah.

"Okay, I mean, if we are going to get married . . . it's really fine." Becca's tone was casual. "I mean, I don't go to church that often anyway."

"Exactly!" said Andreas. "I don't understand how that has anything to do with who comes to the wedding."

It was on again, and the supervision group watched for a couple more minutes as Becca and Andreas bickered about who got to decide who came to the wedding. Isaiah stopped the tape and inquired about how he could have handled the exchange better. As the group began talking about their responses to the couple, Dr. Gonzales was quieter than usual. Several questions were generated, and Isaiah was able to take a few pointers from Sydney, who was in an emotionally focused therapy (EFT) class, about how to de-escalate and increase empathy in the couple. Like Becca, Sydney's parents had divorced when she was young. Amy's parents were still married; her father was a pastor, and her mother a nurse. She experienced their marriage as boring and predictable, not particularly bad but not particularly good.

Dr. Gonzales, also married, let the conversation go on for a bit and then interjected. "You know, Isaiah, I'm wondering whether the conflict is both about who gets to come to the wedding and, perhaps less consciously, showing some inner conflict on Becca's part about giving up her Catholic faith. What do you think?"

"Yeah, maybe," said Isaiah, "but she didn't seem to think it was a big deal."

Dr. Gonzales turned to the group: "How is everyone feeling about Becca's process of converting to Islam in this context?" The question, while not directly related to the clinical question Isaiah brought up, was not something the group could ignore. Given Dr. Gonzales's power as the professor, the group members shifted focus. As the conversation started, it became clear that Amy and Sydney had not even paid much attention to the issue; they were consumed with what they experienced as unfair pressure on Becca regarding the wedding attendees. Isaiah, feeling like he may have missed something in the material, was circumspect about the conversion. He said he had thought about it a little, but since it was something that Becca had decided to do, he was not sure there was anything more he should explore except her feelings of unfairness. She was, after all, freely choosing to marry Andreas. Amy agreed, but Sydney was less sure.

Dr. Gonzales was internally distressed. Being raised a Catholic Christian herself, she was currently attending a nondenominational church and felt herself pondering the gravity of conversion to Islam. She wondered whether the ramifications of Becca's decision were weightier than anyone was acknowledging. She went on to point out that religious conversions were not just temporal matters and that Catholicism and Islam were incommensurable traditions (i.e., you couldn't be both). What were the long-term implications of Becca converting to Islam? What did everyone believe?

Isaiah was also Christian; he had been raised in the church, and he and his family were Methodist. He attended church a lot when he was a kid, but when he started college, he sort of stopped. After he and his wife had children, they thought about reengaging in church, but their attendance was sporadic, and there wasn't a lot of space in his life for meaningful spirituality. Sydney had grown up in a small, conservative Pentecostal church, and the strictness of her home and church had left her with little room for exploration. After college she had moved away and was currently not attending any church. Amy considered herself spiritual but not religious. Despite growing up attending church every Sunday, her current allegiance to her faith was uncertain. She mostly kept this quiet, especially from her parents, as she did not want to upset her father.

As the group continued to discuss Dr. Gonzales's question, it became clear that she was the only one who seemed to think the question was worth discussing with Becca and Andreas. Isaiah pushed back, worrying that he would be introducing his own agenda. This wasn't even something they were seeking help to resolve. Amy thought it would be intrusive to bring it up, and she knew some mixed-faith couples who seemed to do okay. Sydney was not sure what to think or say, recalling a boy in high school whom her parents forbade her to date because he was Catholic.

DOMAINS OF DEVELOPMENT

By now you are familiar with our emphasis on the emergent, nonlinear, and fluid nature of clinical integration. The integrative moment, a *kairos* moment, occurs within the context of therapist and client, each bringing their unique self and experiences to the clinical/counseling relationship as it unfolds moment by moment.[1] As such, as we know from our discussion about tradition, we do not arrive at this relationship absent history. In Donnel Stern's (2017) words, we enter each clinical experience "with all the reverberations of the past built right into those present moments" (p. 82). Therefore, as we invited you earlier to consider your traditions and ethics, in this chapter we are inviting you to more deeply contemplate the complexity of your personal experience and how this experience has shaped you up to this point in your life. Consider your personal reactions to the supervision session described above. Whom did you most identify with and why? What were you saying to yourself as you were reading the back and forth between Dr. Gonzales and her supervisees? What emotions or memories did this case study evoke for you? Was there any hardening of your opinions? Did you find yourself becoming a tad judgmental or disinterested or excited?

This chapter is about the particularity of how our traditions and ethics give rise to the unique stamp of our hermeneutical process. In other words, understanding our tradition and ethical frame is important to grasping how these factors influence our contribution to the integrative experience. However, we do not simply *know* our tradition and ethics. As we have argued, tradition and ethics are deep affective processes that we inhabit and embody. Consequently, this type of knowing is inseparable from our respective developmental histories and the various relationships and communal settings that formed or shaded our distinctive expression of these traditions and values. For instance, it would be difficult to separate Isaiah, Dr. Gonzales, Amy, and Sydney's reactions from their genders, cultures, races, ethnicities, religious traditions, and so on.

---

[1] *Kairos* is a Greek word referring to a right or critical moment.

But that doesn't quite go far enough. It is not only, for instance, that Dr. Gonzales is a Catholic Mexican immigrant or that Amy is an African American Protestant. The distinct intersection of these factors is individualized in the lives of Dr. Gonzales and Amy, making their stories personal and intimate.

More than simply answering questions about where we are from or what we know about ourselves, we have recently been challenged to think about *"Where do we know from?"* This question, originating in the work of Black feminist Katherine McKittrick and expanded by Eugenia Zuroski (2020), aims to decenter our knowledge from dominant cultural narratives and help us think deeply about the personally situated and culturally saturated locations of our knowledge. Identifying where one is speaking from allows room for people whose stories are not reflected in the Western cultural assumptions that may dominate how we think about our own progress and personal lives. For instance, it would be difficult for Dr. Gonzales or Amy to speak about their development fully if they were not allowed to identify how being Mexican or African American in a White-majority culture shapes how they understand themselves as clinicians and the problems their clients face. Their social location is inextricably entangled in all aspects of their life, affecting each domain of integration.

So, while we gather general information by thinking about intersectional categories, understanding the personal stories of our group participants helps us appreciate their motivations and how each member brings their own specific version of what it's like to be the daughter of a Black pastor, a White female growing up in a fundamentalist-leaning Pentecostal church, a lapsed Methodist, or a counseling psychologist from a Mexican immigrant family. These unique experiences are why knowing a specific client is always more complex than merely knowing about a client's cultural, ethnic, or religious group. Moreover, the influence between unique developmental contexts and one's religious tradition is not a one-way, linear process. Rather, the engagement between developmental processes and religious tradition is reciprocal, entangled, overdetermined, and irreducibly complex; we'll talk more about this as we progress through the chapter. Yet highlighting the influence of developmental processes on clinically integrative practice allows counselors and therapists a deeper understanding of their individual clients and how faith uniquely operates in each therapeutic relationship. To accomplish this task, we will talk about three intertwined domains or processes that shape development: personal history, theoretical/professional pathways, and spiritual or religious formation.

Personal history. When we refer to *personal history*, we are speaking about the emotional and relational environment you and your client have each experienced throughout life, as a child, adolescent, and all stages of adulthood. Think about the structure of your intimate relationships, your family, and how that has changed over the years. What about the presence of illnesses, losses to death, delays/disruptions in physical or sexual development, or gender identity? Consider the presence of trauma and how that has affected emotional ties. What about the nature of attachments and the level of enmeshment verses differentiation? Are there any relational fractures and cutoffs? Reflect on environmental influences such as loss of employment, economic instability or lack of resources, natural disasters, immigration, racial and ethnic violence, moving, health care access, housing, and food stability. If you think about the material covered in a standard clinical interview or when you construct a genogram or trauma timeline, you will capture some of what we are talking about. In these experiences we are being shaped or formed in particular ways that order who we are as clinicians.

While it is no doubt helpful to understand various theoretical perspectives when thinking about development, we like Marion Milner's (2011) suggestion that we not "force the self into a theory" (p. 62). Instead, following the lead of Esther Thelen and Linda Smith (1994), we recognize the open and dynamic nature of developmental processes, where qualities of emergence, mutual influence, and nonlinearity are inherently present during all of development. As we hinted at in chapter one, becoming a person is filled with surprises, good fortune, twists and turns, jerky movements, trauma, catastrophes, serendipity, and do-overs. Echoing Tronick (2007, 2022; Tronick & Beeghly, 2011), this open developmental systems approach rests on the assumption that we are *fundamentally* active meaning makers from birth. As we develop, we are continually and iteratively making meaning of our experience, good and bad, which in turn forms our sense of self in relation to the world and other people. Beginning with preverbal affective experience, as development progresses we accumulate increasingly sophisticated ways of understanding our world. Registering both explicitly in conscious thought and more complexly in procedural personal/social unconscious processes, by the time we reach adulthood we have, hopefully and at least for the most part, learned how to navigate our way through life.

While this may seem obvious by this point in our argument, we highlight these qualities of individual history to reemphasize that our personal experience as therapists contributes to the distinctiveness of every therapeutic relationship. Three areas of consideration follow as we turn the focus of examination from the client to the clinician.

First is the importance of paying attention to thwarted or derailed aspects of our development because something happened when it shouldn't have (intrusion) or, conversely, nothing happened when it should have (deprivation). While everyone has experienced disappointment and expectable failures due to the normal range of parenting/caretaking inadequacies, sometimes these failures repeat often enough or are severe enough to adversely affect and distort how we organize and make meaning of our emotional and relational lives. For instance, in the case study at the beginning of this chapter, we can imagine the responses from Amy and Sydney, while superficially similar, are actually distinct narratives emerging from two different emotional and relational histories. Neither Amy nor Sydney may have consciously picked up on the interfaith struggle, but for different reasons. Further, Dr. Gonzales clearly made meaning of the fight between Andreas and Becca differently from Isaiah. She picked up on the possible displaced/disavowed anger and guilt on the part of Becca, who was being asked to abandon her Catholic tradition. This insight, if it proves to be accurate, cannot be separated from Dr. Gonzales's own experience as a Catholic immigrant who converted to Protestantism. Each of these distinct histories, including Isaiah's, contributes to how they think about getting married and the notion of difference in marriage.[2]

Second, we must attend to the presence of protective factors in our development and how these have allowed us to flourish or

---

[2]As discussed in chapter four, we realize this tilt in our conversation may bring up the topic of therapist/counselor values. However, we do not have space or time to speak to the vast array of issues and concerns regarding the influence of therapist/counselor values in the clinical relationship. For our purposes we want to echo our stance that any therapeutic relationship inherently involves moral discourse from which there is no escape (Cushman, 1995). In addition, our view of the clinical relationship as irreducibly intersubjective means that therapist/counselor values will inevitably affect the direction and nature of the treatment at both conscious and unconscious levels. Therefore (in agreement with Bland et al., 2018), we see any discussion of the eradication, suspension, and/or bracketing of counselor values within the therapeutic relationship as problematic and unrealistic in any meaningful clinical exchange. In our opinion, the discussion of therapist/counselor values should center on the need for all clinicians to explore, identify, and understand their own emotional, relational, and communal context and histories in order to develop a robust capacity to regulate their own therapeutic ambitions, particularly those that may border on dominating or negating the priority of an asymmetrical focus on the client's process and freedom. The appropriate degree to which therapists and counselors directly articulate their values in the treatment is dependent on the unique circumstances of each clinical relationship.

engage life in adaptive and productive ways. Understanding the range and nature of our own advantages and privileges (e.g., safe and supportive communities, economic stability, health care, responsive parents, racial/ethnic majority, healthy faith community) gives us insight into the way we think about healthy functioning, the expectancies we bring regarding what is possible for our clients to achieve, and notions of proper and improper ways of operating in the world. Here, as we discussed in chapter four, we see the formation of our ethical sensibilities, the expectations we bring regarding what is possible for our clients to achieve, and notions of proper and improper ways of operating in the world. As Malin Fors (2018) aptly describes, sometimes the intersection of these privileges varies from client to client. Sometimes we are more advantaged than the client, sometimes less, and sometimes we are in similar states of advantage or disadvantage within a given social context.

Likewise, all therapists and counselors have assumptions, not always conscious, about how to achieve positive outcomes, belief in what is true, or what passes for a good life outcome. If, as mental health professionals, we are to mine our ethics, as we have encouraged you to do, then when we think about what is good or true in the process of human growth and flourishing, we have to pay attention to truth and goodness as representations in our mind, what might be a true or good outcome for ourselves and a client, and how truth and goodness are understood in the process of therapy (see chapter two for this discussion). In other words, clinical work is more about process than content, even if our vision of a healthy horizon is shared with those we treat (e.g., that a good life should involve freedom of choice or emotional awareness), how this is achieved in our client's life may diverge significantly from our own experience. Here, overlapping with our discussion of theoretical ethics in chapter four, we must remember that our ideas about what we personally value as a good outcome are influenced by the ethical priorities that emerge from the theories we choose to guide our work.

The third aspect of personal development is related to specific traumatic events or circumstances in our lives and how these have acquainted us with catastrophe, loss, unspeakable pain, or unintelligible suffering. These tragic circumstances may be characterized both as intrusive trauma, which may break into otherwise normal life experience, and/or insidious trauma that is deeply embedded in the very nature of early relational organizations. This latter form are the traumas where there is *no before*.[3] Perhaps, as Ed Tronick (2022) points out, the use of the word *trauma* (suggestive of discrete or static events) is not the best in cases where intrusion and depravation are chronic and severe. In these situations, there may be traumatic events—occurrences of physical or sexual abuse—but they are starkly disturbing events within a chronically insidious nonempathic and nonresponsive relational context where no meaning can be made (Cates, 2014). Here, there is no choice but to muster our defenses, of whatever sort may be effective (dissociation, denial, acting out, splitting, etc.), to protect ourselves from overwhelming and unintelligible affect. Identifying the signs and whispers of our trauma may be accomplished by identifying areas of rigidity in our responsiveness, the lack or loss of ability to mentalize the experience of others, contexts in which we experience significant emotional dysregulation, and the ways we act out behaviorally. While these are just a few of the potential indicators of trauma, understanding the ways our personal trauma shapes the organization of our relational and emotional life will go a long way to help us effectively attune and respond to our client's traumas.

---

[3] By *no before*, we are referring to situations where development occurs in chronically disturbed environment. There was never a time of normalcy.

Because developmental opportunities, failures, and traumatic events affect our growth in ways that are both evident and hidden, our client's history may contrast or converge with our own experiences—shaping the nature of treatment transferences and enactments. Here we find the perfect context for moments of integration as we work to identify God's healing power in the very mechanisms of what has historically been seen as the negative or problematic aspects of treatment—countertransference enactments. While certainly transference entanglements can threaten, derail, or minimize the progress and effectiveness of treatment, this is also the territory of powerful change and healing. Remember, our transference reactions to clients are not always based on similar experiences (e.g., death of a parent) but more likely on analogous emotional experiences that may emerge from very different situations. For example, when thinking about marriage and faith, each of our group participants has a transference response to Andreas and Becca that emerges from their own histories.

Being aware of how we as therapists are activated allows us to think about the client rather than repeat our own struggle with the client, which often takes the form of unconsciously trying to heal ourselves by healing our client. Here you will see that our idea of integration is closely tied to how we think about change and what is the most effective form of therapeutic action—something we will specifically get into in the next section. For now, let us hold the idea that God's healing intention is immanently present and mobilized within the therapeutic—read transference—relational processes of our clinical work, both in the life of the client and in our lives.

Theoretical/professional pathways. The second area of development is what we are calling *theoretical or professional pathways*. Most of us wondered at one time or another why it is that we chose this impossible profession. Of the many vocations available to us, we have chosen to be deeply involved in the troubles and pain of humanity. While many aspects of our vocation are rewarding and meaningful, it is difficult to become involved in the complexities and tragedies of our clients' lives without being affected. Our acquaintance with loss, grief, trauma, and irreconcilable heartbreak is sometimes acute, and chronic exposure to this work can take its toll on our lives. We say this not as a discouragement; rather, like many of you, we have found profound meaning and purpose in the therapeutic engagement of human suffering. We are convinced that our work contributes to the liberation of humanity from the devastations of sin and moves us toward loving-kindness, freedom, and justice—proclaiming the kingdom of God. However, if we drill down to the various influences that have shaped our vocational choice, we need to consider the level of personal motivation. What is it about this profession that motivated you/us to commit long hours and lots of money? One way to think about this is to consider what type of problem this profession solves for us. Or perhaps, how is this profession involved in our search for self-understanding and healing, or an attempt to heal someone close to us? What narcissistic needs does it satisfy, or how do aspects of this profession repeat familiar patterns of suffering?

You can see here that we are searching not only for an intellectual answer, although this is important; we are also looking for emotional motivations and how these may influence our choice to become a clinician and more specifically how we behave at any given point in session with a client. Sometimes we are very conscious of our emotional motivations; at other times they are hidden, and we only find ourselves, and how we think and feel about what we are doing, as we engage our client's experience (Sussman, 2007).

For instance, if we think about Dr. Gonzales for a minute, we could wonder how aware she is about her reactivity to the client's experience of conversion. While it is certainly theoretically justifiable to help a client elaborate all dimensions of their emotional experience, especially when facing big decisions, she is the only one in the group who focused on Becca's experience of converting from Catholicism to Islam. How might her own experience of conversion be operating as a motivating influence to highlight this experience for her students? Here we can imagine that what might be stirring Dr. Gonzales, at least to some degree, is not only her ethics or theological tradition. It is possible that she experiences an unconscious, distressing reactivation of the emotional and relational turmoil related to changing from Catholicism, which was entrenched deeply in her Mexican heritage, to evangelical Protestantism.

Further, in our work as professors who teach and supervise clinical work, we find that personal motivation is important to the direction students and candidates take in this field. Some move toward hospital work or private practice, or want to concentrate working with a specific population, such as the severely mentally ill, children, families, or veterans. More than once we have found that students move toward or shy away from certain areas of this field based on very personal feelings or inclinations that they may not be able to fully articulate. Even those who have spent several years in the profession often pivot the emphasis of their clinical work based on very personal experiences or developmental shifts that occur due to age, professional pressures and questions, or life experience. This doesn't strike us as problematic, as we discussed in chapter two; it simply speaks to the person of the therapist as critical to what happens with the client. Reflecting on our personal reasons helps us clarify our hopes, fears, perceptions, and expectations of our profession.

Additionally, as we think about our personal motivations for engaging in the field of mental health, this also includes the different education pathways people have taken (e.g., clinical, counseling, or school psychology, marriage and family therapy, professional counseling, social work, pastoral counseling). Where and how we are trained frequently overlaps with the specific theories or methods we become comfortable using when working with our clients. Although we have received training in several different modalities, we lean psychoanalytic in our work. Alternatively, you may find yourself drawn to family systems, cognitive-behavioral, emotion-focused, shorter term, or more directive approaches. Moreover, in their definitive work *Faces in a Cloud*, George Atwood and Robert Stolorow (1993) clearly demonstrate how our subjective personality organization is deeply connected to the theories we rely on to explain clinical experience. Whatever your preference, we believe it is important to consider what draws you to certain ways of thinking about and being with clients.

Because this is an intensely personal field and clinical work in general regularly engages our emotions, often at deep levels, we are further shaped by our professors and supervisors, who are invested in helping us learn a certain way of being a clinician. The formative power of our instructors and supervisors is so personal, intimate, and intense that we often find ourselves identifying or even idealizing certain individuals whom we want to emulate or copy. It is also interesting that those who have sought their own personal therapy (something we believe is vital for working as a clinician) find that their experience in therapy helps shape who they are as a professional, not just in the ways of understanding life better but in the adoption of a more personal method of relating therapeutically. As we hinted at in previous chapters, we develop as clinicians by learning and reading about how to practice, being shaped by our supervisors, experiencing what it's like to be in counseling/therapy, and hanging around other professionals who are doing this work. It is what Polanyi (1958) describes as the accumulation of tacit knowledge.

To summarize this section so far, our professional and theoretical pathways are shaped by personal experiences and motivations that entangle our traditions and ethics. Further, as our professional identity develops, this personal history influences the type of clinical training we pursue and perhaps the type of population or clinical environment in which we want to work. Certain theorists, theoretical ideas, and clinical modalities find us because of our classwork, professors, supervisors, therapists, and the clients we work with. Directly and indirectly, all these sources swirl and merge in our development, hopefully providing a sufficient understanding of what works in therapy and counseling, or how we believe our work leads to meaningful change and growth. Our understanding of therapeutic action, what we think of as really working in therapy, is not only based in our theoretical knowledge but also has deeply subjective and experiential roots. To put it another way, we all form, whether clear and articulate or murky and uncertain, an idea of what helps people get better, and these ideas cannot be separated from our personal and professional developmental processes. Consequently, however sophisticated (or not) it may be, we operate out of our personally informed theory of therapeutic action as we deliberately engage our clients.

Perhaps it is here where you might think about your understanding of therapeutic action and draw linkages to your specific faith tradition (chapter three) and how it has developed in your life. For example, we believe the most powerful processes in the work of therapy involve the provision of a relational experience that allows our clients to develop a new sense of freedom and understanding about themselves, their lives, and the causes of their troubles. Critical to this understanding is the ability for clients to consciously and unconsciously reorganize their emotional/relational experience and responses. This can be accomplished in numerous ways, as various theories will suggest, but we and many others argue that an essential feature of this process is immediacy—where the client and therapist experience the relational and emotional difficulties, whatever they may be, in real time and work them through.

In other words, we can't think our way into change; we must experience the messiness of *changing* together. The most opportune place for this is directly with the counselor/therapist. Because change often involves engaging the counselor in the deep emotional movements of the client's life, therapists who are firmly aware of and mine their subjective experiences and vulnerabilities are better equipped to navigate the oft turbulent waters of transference. Moreover, as clinical integrative practitioners, how we feel successful in our work with clients often depends on our ability to find a connection or echo between how we inhabit the formation elements of our theology and culture as they meaningfully link to our ideas of therapeutic action. We will talk about this more in the next section, but essentially, we believe that our personal development and the influences that shaped our professional direction are not the result of random, incoherent developmental processes but are better understood as potentially meaningful events and progressions that contribute to the unique possibilities we each respectively bring to the field. In other words, as we live into the God-given desires of our hearts, we fit and function well into the revelation of God as it is manifested through our being and our work. Recognizing that this last statement might be seen by some as advocating a sort of Western, emancipated individualism, please hear that we believe considering the uniqueness of our individual development is always grounded in relationality. Echoing Stanley

Grenz (2001), we see the essence of the image of God as "persons-in-community" (p. 31).

Spiritual/religious formation. The final aspect of development we consider is *spiritual/religious formation*. While there have been different ways to think about religious/spiritual development (Carpenter, 2020, Dowling & Scarlett, 2006; Fowler, 2000; Haugen, 2018; Leclerc & Maddix, 2011; Willard, 2002) we suggest the word *formation* better captures what we want to highlight in this dimension of personal experience. Briefly, formation speaks to the specific motivational or causal dimension of spiritual growth and development. Following directives in Scripture, the Christian tradition has always been preoccupied with processes and practices of spiritual development and growth: "Instead, grow in the grace and knowledge of our Lord and savior Jesus Christ" (2 Peter 3:18 CEB); "So let's press on to maturity, by moving on from the basics about Christ's word" (Hebrews 6:1 CEB); "The one who started a good work in you will stay with you to complete the job" (Philippians 1:6 CEB).

Growing into Christ is a bedrock assumption; we seek meaning, purpose, and direction in relationship with the divine. Therefore, essential to this process of formation, or transformation, into the likeness of Christ is our cooperative engagement with the transcendent and immanent work of the Holy Spirit. For Christian traditions broadly speaking, it is the Spirit who works in us, shaping and forming us. And, while we are not the initiators of this work, establishing a formation mindset toward the possibilities of God being present in our work, as we discussed in chapter one, attunes us to anticipate emergent experiences of God's presence in the deeply human domains of emotion and desire (Zahl, 2020).

Space does not permit a thorough review of all that has been written on this topic, so our discussion will lack some nuance and sophistication, but we want to suggest an understanding of spiritual formation as the process of *maturing toward and within* a mindset that orders one's life around expressions of love toward God, self, and others in our daily lives. No doubt, as you reviewed your faith tradition back in chapter three, you were able to identify specific ways you have been taught to deepen or nurture your faith. These probably included different spiritual disciplines or practices that are seen as critical for growth in Christ. Although these may vary across traditions, in our reading of the different practices many features seem common across differing perspectives that mark the formation process as distinctly Christian. In this section we will briefly outline some common features of spiritual formation, discuss how these processes may engage our clinical experience, and share some thoughts about why we consider psychotherapy/counseling as unique within the many practices we can use to grow spiritually.

Describing the common elements of the spiritual formation process starts with a shared understanding that the experience of maturing in Christ is transformational in the sense that we are living into what we have not yet been or experienced. In other words, the process is continually aspirational, to be *Christlike*, something that in our fallen state will never be fully realized in this life. Somewhat paradoxically, then, while spiritual formation is aspirational, it can only be achieved through a deep surrender and lack of hurry, worry, moralizing guilt, or condemnation. It is fundamentally a relational process with God. Angela Carpenter (2020) reminds us that we are formed "in openness and response to this relationship" (p. 149). The formation is the *love work* of the Spirit within us, bringing us into alignment with the person of Christ.

Importantly, what makes spiritual formation for the Christian different from other religions is that life for the Christian is "participation in the life of God and in his presence" (Zimmerman, 2012, p. 266). It is not captured in the naive question, *What would Jesus do?* Rather, as Jens Zimmerman explains, formation in Christ requires a deep engagement of the gospel in one's culture. This is an act of interpretation to participate in the reality of who we are and the contexts in which we find ourselves. Spiritual formation is never individualistic; its purpose or telos is to realize that our singularity before God is inextricably entangled in our communal/relational presence and responsibility (Brown & Strawn, 2012; Strawn & Brown, 2020). However, the process is no doubt facilitated as we practice certain disciplines or habits and gain more knowledge about Christ. But, as Simeon Zahl (2020) successfully points out, relying on habits, disciplines, and knowledge alone has proven wholly insufficient for the meaningful shaping of the inner character. Instead, there must be an engagement with affective processes of emotion, feeling, and desire.

This brief description sets the table for how we might think about our spiritual formation in relation to our clinical work. As previously discussed, psychotherapy/counseling may have several very practical goals—less distressing emotion, improving mood, reducing interpersonal conflict, more engagement with work, life goals, and so on. But acknowledging only these practical outcomes represents a reductive view of our work because it neglects that we are fully human subjects made in the image of God. We do not work with bodies or minds that are somehow separate from the purposes and will of God in the world. We, as Ben Witherington (2004) describes, are "apart from God . . . the chief actors in the drama of redemption" (p. 223). And this redemption is not just our redemption or growth but that of the people we encounter. Not to be confused with other roles or functions within the body of Christ (Hathaway & Yarhouse, 2021), our clinical work creates a unique and vital opportunity to participate in the expansion of God's kingdom in the realm of intimate relating. As therapists, we are facilitators and coparticipants in the cultivation of the work of the Spirit in our lives and those of our clients.

In previous work (Bland & Strawn, 2014) we argued that psychoanalytic psychotherapy or any therapy/counseling in general could, and often should, be considered a method of spiritual formation. This point has been made in various forms by other authors who are interested in the intimate connection between the spiritual life of the therapist and how this affects clinical work (e.g., Benner, 1988; Coe & Hall, 2010; Olthuis, 2001; Steere, 1997; White, 2020). As we think about how this might work specifically in the intersubjective space of therapy, we suggest that our spiritual formation includes the working out of our spiritual development as we encounter pain, sin, or suffering in our clients. Regardless of the faith experience of those we work with, the formative influence of the Spirit is not only working in our lives as individuals but also emerges within the relational connections we have with our clients.

Here we can see where the value of spiritual disciplines and practices make sense as a method of staying connected to the Spirit, who holds us in our work. This may prove difficult for some of us who experienced calls to growth in Christ not as an invitation to participate in love but as demanding rules or rigid expectations about how good Christians should conduct themselves. Religious experiences of rigid moralizing often create resistance or feelings of guilt or inadequacy about how we are conducting our Christian life. It makes the task of spiritual formation, that of coming to know the voice of Jesus, difficult to tease out from more destructive messages we may have internalized over the years. Addressing this problem, Gary Moon (1997) has a nice way of differentiating the voice of the Jesus from the many internalized messages of shame and condemnation we may have absorbed during childhood. Moon says that the invitation of Jesus is never condemning; it does not play on our fears or anxieties about the future, does not load us down with burdensome expectations, and Christ's corrections are specifically tailored to our life and context; they are never global or shaming. Thinking about this in the clinical realm, it may be interesting to identify times we have lost touch with the invitational nature of spiritual formation and begun to think about or respond to our clients from a relational position that communicates shame, unattainable expectations, or anxiousness.

SUMMARY AND QUESTIONS FOR CONSIDERATION

In this chapter we have encouraged you to personalize your journey as a means of forming the mindset of an integrative clinician. If we think about our case example at the beginning of the chapter, we may begin to wonder what God is up to in each of the participants' lives, not just to determine a clinical strategy for the client but to see how this clinical experience is inviting all the participants to grow in Christlikeness. What aspect of her own conversion is God inviting Dr. Gonzales to explore? How might the Spirit be working with Isaiah in the gentle confrontation about his disavowal of a critical component of Becca's identity? What level of bidding is present for Amy and Sydney? Is there an invitation for them to examine anger, resentment, or loss with regard to their own experience of Christianity?

Because we believe clinical integration is an emergent property of the therapeutic relationship, integrative moments will inevitably be organized through our personal experience as we relate to our clients' lives and therapeutic process. Cultivating this emergent process requires that we attune ourselves emotionally and relationally, not just to the client but to the emerging aspects of our own experience as we engage with clinical work. We can understand our personal experience during development as shaping the distinctive profile we bring to each clinical relationship. Our faith, ethics, and theoretical assumptions are never disembodied realties; they live within and become animated in our responses to each clinical moment. This does not mean that our way of understanding clients, our hermeneutics, is singular or unrelatable; rather, because it is stamped with our personal knowledge and experience, we are able to see ourselves as fully human in a world of humans or as an incarnational human (Zimmerman, 2012). In this way, simultaneous to our provision and facilitation of the Spirit's healing work in our clients, their process will often invite us to reexamine and rework our vulnerabilities, or to address for the first time unprocessed parts of our personal experience and failings. We may find that we grow with our clients.

- As you think about Eugenia Zuroski's question—*Where do we know from?*—what specifically comes to mind in terms of your own development? Think about the unique aspects of your family and how they expressed different cultural or ethnic priorities.

- What have been the major theoretical influences in your approach to clinical work? Consider what might be some of the personal reasons you are drawn to the theories or the clinical emphases you have chosen.

- Because clinical work can be personally activating as we get into the emotional lives of our clients, what types of emotional exchanges do you find most challenging? For instance, is it when you disagree with a client? What about when you feel angry or afraid or attracted to your client?

- In a follow-up to that question, how might you manage these feelings to work effectively with your client, not denying their presence but using them to lean in to what might be happening clinically?

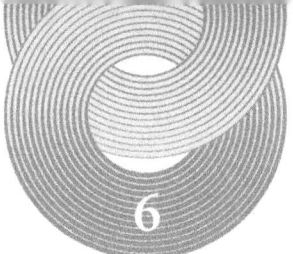

RESILIENCE MATTERS
THE HERMENEUTICS OF NOURISHING EMERGENCE

Thus far we have started every chapter in this book with a clinical supervision scenario that attempts to get you, our dialogue partner, to step into the world of clinical integration as it actually happens—in therapeutic relationships. If we have been successful, you have witnessed how the processes and questions related to clinical integration don't start in the domains of theology, philosophy, or abstract theory but in the emotionally fraught world of relational connection and self-experience. Consequently, each of our clinical stories comes directly from our experience over decades of clinical work, supervision, and teaching on integration. Hopefully you can relate to these cases, but some may be more unique and reflect the lives and journeys of us as the authors. You, of course, will have your own stories that challenge you in the particularity of your life and clinical work. We say this because we have both spent a lot of time preoccupied with the question, How do we live our lives in faithful allegiance to our Christian faith while practicing what we believe to be one of the most powerful disciplines, capable of bring healing and flourishing to a fallen and fragmented humanity? Our stories and clinical focus necessarily arise from this concern.

Stated more simply, *understanding what God is up to in our clinical work* is the reason we pursue integration. Moreover, while we recognize this question has personal, professional, and cultural roots, it has also been deeply shaped by the forces of intellectual history that make such an integration project relevant and vital for Christian mental health workers.[1] As many reflections on the history of thought show, our modern understanding of the human condition is fragmented and siloed. Most tragically, what we know and believe about human behavior and functioning has in large part been actively dis-integrated from our religious faith and a meaningful understanding of God. Consequently, it has become normal for many Christians to learn about the world, the humanities, and the sciences absent a deep and meaningful conversation with what we know about God theologically and experientially. While this is a problem for all the disciplines, from law and business, to sociology and education, to physics and biology, our concern is how it takes shape in the field of psychology, counseling, and clinical practice. Opinions vary as to the success and or validity of our pursuit, but we do not despair this process. We believe the field of psychology has revealed invaluable truths about the nature of humans, human relationships, and how we might better address the problems of human suffering. These truths are not antithetical to scriptural revelation but merely reflect God's voice as he speaks from the book of creation.

In addition, we also recognize that the current stream of integration literature to which we are speaking has often been a preoccupation of the White, Reformed, evangelical Christian Western world. This is not because people of color, diverse ethnicities, other Christian traditions, sexual minorities, and other diverse people

---

[1] A more complete articulation of these important theoretical, philosophical, and historical processes has been well documented in previous waves of integration literature.

groups are uninterested. Rather, it appears the dominant voices of majority culture have been slow to prioritize how this conversation might look from those whose experience is not adequately captured by the majority perspective publishing world. A recent discussion by Dwiwardani & Whitney (2022), confronting the hermeneutical injustice in much of integration scholarship, points to the glaring oversight in integration literature that misses culturally embedded context.[2] This is particularly evident when different cultures and communities have "embodied ways of integrating faith and spirituality [that] have not always been formally called 'integration' per se" (p. 238). Their cyclical model of cultural integration is enormously helpful. Thankfully, there are several other efforts to broaden this conversation, and we hope that some of the processes of reflection and engagement we outline in this book are helpful by framing a method for considering the particularity of each clinical relationship.[3]

To that end, this chapter speaks to resilience in the pursuit of integration. In previous work (Strawn et al., 2018), we suggested that resilience for the integrative clinician "is not just about therapist self-care or growth, but the cultivation of an attitude of expectancy and wonder regarding the unique and unpredictable ways God may manifest his presence in therapy and counseling relationships" (p. 92). We further advocated that integrative clinicians would benefit from practices that foster an attitude of

---

[2] We appreciate Dwiwardani & Whitney (2022) for highlighting the work of Fricker (2007) who defined hermeneutical injustice as occurring "when a gap in collective interpretative resources puts someone at an unfair disadvantage when it comes to making sense of their social experiences" (p. 1)

[3] For instance, both the *Journal of Psychology and Christianity* (Vazquez & Knabb, 2023) and the *Journal of Psychology and Theology* (Strawn & Bland, 2018) have published special issues regarding integration and race, highlighting minority voices. Mark Yarhouse (e.g., 2019; Yarhouse & Sadusky, 2022) has published extensively on the topic of sexual minorities, and there are others who have addressed various themes related to diversity and faith, e.g., McNeil (2005, 2010), Fisher (2021), Reed (2024), Sandage and Strawn (2022), Vazquez et al. (2023), and Whitney et al. (2023).

expectancy and "keep us on the edge of our seats with regards to what God is up to" (p. 92). Once again, we return to Gadamer's (1975) radical call for the highest good in a hermeneutical enterprise to be one of openness and curiosity. We suggest that practices that benefit Christian therapists will include activities that keep us open, expectant, and keen to observe how God is present in our work, in our own lives, and most critically in the lives of our clients. To set the stage, what follows is a brief framework of how we might understand the presence of the Holy Spirit in our clinical work. This is followed by a discussion of resilience proper as it relates to the type of spirituality we might want to foster as we work to stay attuned to what God is up to in our clinical relationships.

WHERE IS THE SPIRIT?

Throughout this book we have been speaking about *integrative moments*, the emergent phenomena of God showing up in a clinical experience that cannot be wholly dictated or predicted by our theories or techniques. At the same time, however, these moments are deeply influenced and reliant on the dynamic and complex subjectivities of the therapist and client. In some ways this seems to indicate that there is something unique or singular about the integrative moment that distinguishes it from other clinical experiences. In response we want to say, of course, yes. Emergent integrative moments are powerful transcendent moves of the Spirit that engage us in extraordinary ways. However, we also want to say no. Integrative moments are happening all the time through the healing immanent work of God as it is expressed in the everyday therapeutic processes we all practice.

So how can this be: How can we say yes and no? This seeming contradiction is one way of considering what theology often refers to as general versus special revelation. God reveals God's self in the wonder and grandeur of the natural created world, and he has specifically revealed himself through Scripture, the person of Jesus Christ, miracles, prophecy—phenomena that are outside the ordinary work of God that sustains creation. Thankfully, previous waves of integration have addressed this question from numerous angles, so for our purposes we would like to briefly identify four dimensions of this *seeming* duality that will help clarify what we mean when we talk about the role of the Spirit in the integrative moment. These include the entangled nature of God's transcendent and immanent presence in the world, anticipating spiritual experience, the uniqueness of a Christian clinical perspective, and a practical framework for recognizing the Holy Spirit in clinical work.

Transcendence and immanence. "Our world is disenchanted," says social psychologist Richard Beck (2021, p. 21). He's not alone in this view. In his highly influential work *A Secular Age*, philosopher Charles Taylor (2007) describes the modern self as *buffered*, meaning we have so thoroughly adopted the modern scientific mindset that we are almost impervious to thinking about powers beyond the natural order, in the realm of the transcendent, spiritual, or mysterious. It was not always this way; in previous centuries, the enchantment of the spiritual and mysterious was always close at hand.

For instance, as psychologists, counselors, and therapists we all have a rather sophisticated understanding of how the human mind works, how it goes wrong, and various methods to help get us back on track. Growing out of the scientific advances of the nineteenth and twentieth centuries, clinical practice has become quite sophisticated in addressing the many emotional and relational wounds faced by our clients. What in previous centuries was seen as spiritual oppression in need of divinely supernatural intervention, or divine punishment for infractions of God's commandments, we now understand as the results of trauma, disordered development, biochemical abnormalities, and genetic variances. In many ways prayer, confession, or the laying on of hands, as a means of addressing our emotional ills, has been replaced with psychotherapy, behavioral practices, or medication. Where people once sought healing in the church, they now seek healing in the therapist's office.[4]

These *secular practices*, as they are sometimes called, are available to all who would learn. You do not need to be a Christian or even religious to access the healing powers that exist in the natural order—for example, empathy, relational connection and support, insight, emotional processing, and learning a new behavior or way of coping. This picture, of course, is not as stark as we have just described. Many people of faith still seek healing and solace using spiritual practices and community. However, culturally we have moved from the idea that reality could not be comprehended without God to a reality that seems largely coherent in the absence of God (Taylor, 2007).

We provide this very brief historical reflection on our disenchanted age because we believe it has direct relevance to how we consider divine action in our therapeutic work and how we think about clinically integrative practice. As Grenz and Olson (1992) point out, Christian theology has been engaged in a centuries-old argument about the transcendence and immanence of God. Like these authors, we believe the only reasonable way to understand the work of God in clinical practice is to hold the indissoluble tension between the nature-penetrating works of a self-contained God who exists apart from the world alongside and entangled with a God who is "present to creation, active within the world and involved with the historical and natural processes" (p. 310). In

---

[4]This is by no means a new argument and has been cogently argued by Benner (1988), Taylor (2007), and many others.

other words, our sensitivity to the enchantment of the Spirit as it rests on our work should be as robust as our recognition of the Spirit's movement in the natural processes of emotional healing.

As we stated in previous chapters, part of the problem with grasping the integrative processes in clinical work is that we have often been taught in religious settings that God is mostly present when we consciously invite him into the work through biblical admonitions or encouragements, invoking the name of Jesus, practicing a specific spiritual discipline such as prayer/meditation, or perhaps applying *Christian-accommodative* treatments (Worthington et al., 2013).[5] We are sympathetic to this way of thinking; it is often deeply rewarding when we explicitly and consciously connect to our clients in their spirituality. However, if we limit ourselves to these descriptors of spirituality in the clinical relationship, we run the risk of relying on more declarative or propositional understandings of God than experiential.

In contrast, Simeon Zahl (2020) states that a signature indicator of God's presence in any relational encounter is the activation of affect. More about this later, but for now we suggest that sustaining ourselves as integrative clinicians means developing a sensitivity to the entangled, oscillating presence of spiritual transcendence and immanence, that one is not preferable or even realistically extricable from the other. In fact, what emerges will largely be dependent on the nature of the clinical relationship and work. Importantly, we want to speak against any false dualism regarding God's presence in our clinical practice—this kind of thinking reduces the immanent work of the Spirit to human processes such as empathy or insight, while the transcendent work of God is like a

---

[5]Christian-accommodative treatment refers to a process where therapeutic interventions that have developed without any specific considerations of religion, spirituality, or faith are modified in a manner that would increase their acceptance within specific faith communities—for instance, the use of Scripture as content in a mindfulness intervention for anxiety or stress reduction.

holy infusion, a burning bush, if you will. These distinctions may work for abstract theological descriptions, but they become clunky and constricting in the emotionally undulating, moment-to-moment, experience-near clinical process.

Anticipating spiritual experience. Because the combination of God's immanence and transcendence means that the work of Christ is both *"palpable and elusive"* (Hays, 2020, p. 67, italics original), we are always operating with humility as to the presence and work of God. In addition, we are reluctant to delimit how the Spirit emerges in the therapeutic relationship, and we will avoid any attempt to provide an exhaustive description of spiritual experience. However, we do want to provide some pragmatic handles that may help us grasp how the Spirit's presence becomes evident in clinical work. Therefore, the task is not one of deciphering whether an experience is transcendent or immanent; it is about developing a sensitivity that appreciates the seamless and entangled ways in which God moves in the material world to accomplish his purposes.

Because all relational activities hold together in him, and our experience of God is always mediated through human processes, we do not want to get distracted by metatheoretical questions about whether the Spirit is in some material or natural process. Rather, if we are seeking to understand the work of God, we will be looking more to the direction or aim of the clinical work in contrast to the specifics of how it is being manifested. This takes us out of the abstracted world of theological discussions (Is this an immanent or transcendent expression of the divine?) and into the world of what God is wanting to accomplish in the embodied emotional and relational life of our clients. Of course, there are times when it seems the affective moment in therapy infuses with the numinous—the holy—and we are left with feelings of awe and gratitude, but this is not always or even frequently the case. Perhaps a story will help clarify our intent.

Recently I (Earl) was cruising on the waters off northern British Columbia. At one point a small group of us boarded a Zodiac (a rigid inflatable boat) looking for wildlife. We were able to spot seals, sea lions, a mama bear and her cubs, bald eagles, and numerous other birds. Like most who cruise these waters, we were hoping for a glimpse of a whale's tail or fin. Despite our hope and expectant searching, we collectively gasped in amazement when a pod of orcas surfaced about fifty yards in front of us. Our guide immediately killed the motor, and most of us stood up to watch their majestic fins cutting through the calm surface. We became silent with wonder and awe. They moved on, and we did not see them again, but for the rest of the excursion we were on the edge of our seats in anticipation: Would we see more?

Although distinct from counseling or psychology, Earl's expectant and hopeful experience in the Zodiac is analogous to the spiritual sensitivity and emotional posture we are calling for in clinically integrative practice. Spiritual experience is necessarily subjective, unique to the individual person, and reliant on context. As our analogy suggests, we can be assured that the spiritual dimension of our work is constantly present, moving, and available, even if its more spectacular forms are below the surface, less available for conscious experience. In other words, cultivating a spiritual sensitivity allows us to be present with the more common ways God shows up in our clinical work but also calls us to be on the edge of our seats, watchful for those moments when the divine emerges from deeper waters in extraordinary ways.

Christian spiritual experience in clinical practice. It will be impossible for us to outline the depth and breadth of discussions that have centered on the topic of Christian spiritual experience, so let us narrow our focus to describing a Christian spirituality that is most relevant to clinical practice. In so doing we move away from experience-distant ways of thinking about God and consider how might a God who is embodied, who knows what it is like at every level to be human—how might this God be present in the midst of our work with clients?

To engage in this process, let's remember that "our human experience is the starting point for our imaginations about God" (Halton, 2021, p. 189).[6] This means that our views of God and how God acts in the world are always contextually grounded, which, for Charles Halton, makes them *"functionally real"* (p. 191, italics original). Harking back to chapter two, recall that theology, like clinical practice, is a hermeneutical exercise. It is not a fixed set of propositions or beliefs that we simply cut and paste into our lives. We do theology as we face the demands and challenges of our life, and in our current discussion as we face the task of clinical integration. Therefore, any spirituality in this context must function as real within the frame of a therapeutic relationship. We believe that an emergent clinical imagination of God shifts our focus from generalizations such as transcendence and immanence (concepts useful in teaching and preaching) to the discovery of God within the particular affective/relational experience of clinical work as it is occurring in real time.

Consequently, imagining God, who knows what it is like to be a person, even a person in therapy, means God is intimately acquainted with what it's like to be confused, defensive, traumatized, lost, and ashamed. God has experienced transference enactments and uncertainty about what to say next, has wrestled with unwieldy unconscious motivations, sexuality, and the worry that being God

---

[6]Halton (2021) is not unique in this sentiment, which has been expounded at length by liberation theologians, particularly James Cone (1997, 2011).

may not be enough. This is a God who knows the freedom of releasing past wounds and traumas just as intimately as the maddening frustration of compulsive repetitions.

If we are to work in the gritty, mind-bending complexity of clinical work, we need a spirituality that embraces our full humanity. As David Benner (2011) avers, "The spiritual life should never make you more than, less than, or anything other than fully human" (p. 13). A deeply Christian spirituality doesn't lose divinity but refuses to abstract the humanity of God, to sanitize, minimize, or sanctify the vulnerability and intimacy that Christ experiences with our clients and with us as therapists. If our spirituality is primarily based on our beliefs and takes us away from the embodied experience of what it means to be human, then we are woefully missing the immediacy of God's presence in our clinical work. Eugene Peterson's rendering of Hebrews 4:14-16 helps us here:

> Now that we know what we have—Jesus, this great High Priest with ready access to God—let's not let it slip through our fingers. We don't have a priest who is out of touch with our reality. He's been through weakness and testing, *experienced it all*—all but the sin. So let's walk right up to him and get what he is so ready to give. Take the mercy, accept the help. (MSG, italics added)

This identification, critical to any empathic or therapeutic process, lives in us, through us, and between us as we do the work of counseling and therapy.

Recognizing the work of the Spirit. Given our discussion thus far, we can pull out three obvious characteristics that will help us recognize the Spirit in our work. First, movements of God in therapy and counseling will necessarily be specific to the client, the therapist, and their unique therapeutic relationship. While we all share common humanity, the Spirit's work is exclusive to the context of each therapeutic relationship, which is formed through, not in spite of, our unique developmental histories and traditions.

Therefore, the when, the how, and the what of the Spirit moving is determined by the experiencer—the client and therapist/counselor (Zahl, 2020). While this recognition or conscious awareness may be full, partial, or emerging, we believe that a sensitivity to the unique markers of each therapeutic relationship allows for the anticipation of where and how the Spirit's presence will emerge.

Second, movements of the Spirit will be affectively salient and efficacious. As Zahl (2020) points out, biblical accounts of the moving or presence of the Spirit are frequently connected to the presence of emotion in the subjects of the text. These are not just religious emotions (if we can even use such language) such as awe or transcendence but speak to the full range of emotions available in response to the therapeutic work being done. For instance, the shame and terror experienced by victims of loss or trauma as they work through devastating emotional realities is often a necessary process for healing and growth. Not only are these moments psychically and relationally important, but they are also spiritually rich. Yes, positive affect such as peace, love, joy, and patience gives evidence to the presence of the Spirit, but as we argued in the previous section, this is not only, or even predominantly, where Christ bears witness in our work.

Third, and this may seem obvious when considering the meandering nature of affect in therapy sessions, the work of the Spirit is *"temporally specific"* (Zahl, 2020, p. 76, italics original). This means that evidence of the Spirit is often clear at specific moments in a session or in particular emotional contexts that are being worked through over time. Recall the metaphor of Earl in the Zodiac searching for signs of whales in the water. There is no question the whales are there all the time, but when we come across a particular place in the ocean at a particular time, the whale fin emerges. This is not unlike therapy sessions, which may be predominantly filled with defensive resistance or unintelligible vagueness until there is a shift to insight, emotion, and elaboration. In these moments, emotion presents itself for recognition, reflection, and processing. These are instances that demonstrate God's presence in profound ways, sometimes allowing for awe and wonder. We might even think of these moments as markers, glimpses, or affirmations of the Spirit's constant presence evident in our work.

Before we move on to talk about specific practices that foster resilience in our integrative efforts, we need to make a comment about content and telos. While affective processes, context, and temporal specificity clue us into the emergent presence of the Spirit, we must also remember that the work of God always begins within God's loving and redemptive character. Therefore, the presence of the Spirit will always be characterized by moves toward love, honesty, freedom, justice, hope, faith, self-regulation, and other virtues. There is no law against these things. Clinical work that moves in this direction will inevitably bind itself to truth.

By *truth* we do not mean representational or propositional truth, the notion that we come to realize how and why something is true because of practical experience or rational thought. Rather, as we have mentioned in previous chapters, we are talking about how truth emerges in the empathically attuned relational experience of being seen and validated by an *other*—the therapist. In this therapeutic space both client and counselor can "feel the psychological presence of the other, and the relationship between them feels real ... and in that sense genuine and true" (Allison & Fonagy, 2016, p. 286). This type of connection "generates the felt experience of truth" (p. 287) and builds trust between the therapist and client, which leads to learning and the possibility of change. This intersubjective bond is at the essence of what Todd Hall and Elizabeth Hall (2021) refer to as *relational spirituality* and the intimate roots of transformational change.[7] Again, here we see the entangled presence of the Spirit expressed in the ordinary, and extraordinary, processes of therapeutic work.

RESILIENCE

"Resilience is often born out of a marriage of curiosity and love." In this concise quotation, taken from her book *Still Practicing*, Sandra Buechler (2012, p. 209) captures the spirit we are seeking: the devoted pursuit of understanding within a relational bond characterized by loving-kindness. Fundamentally, this assumes the necessity of pursuing healthy physical and relational exercises, but we believe more specific guidance is needed to foster clinically integrative practice. As we argued above, God is not constrained by the psychological and relational processes described by various theories and techniques of clinical treatment, and our therapies do not dictate the "conditions under which God can show up in the world" (Zimmerman, 2012, p. 285). Therefore, when we talk about resilience in clinical integration, we are speaking to the cultivation of relational, emotional, and spiritual sensibilities that sustain an active and *incarnational* presence as we engage our clients in their suffering. Opening ourselves to the Spirit in this context compels us to consider what specific type of spiritual resilience we need and what realistic steps must we take to achieve our desired end.

What type of spirituality do we need? When our goal is mountain climbing or running a marathon, we can think about the specific type of resilience we might require, things such as breathing capacity, muscular strength, or physical pain tolerance. But in the world of counseling and psychotherapy, we can't think of resilience as some sort of survival skill or simply coping with short-term

---
[7] A similar idea is found in Shults & Sandage (2006).

hardship—a task we engage in for a limited time and, if successful, end with a sense of accomplishment or triumph. Clinical work often does not have a clearly defined route, set of outcomes, or endpoint. We have goals and hopes for the work, but there is always a significant degree of uncertainty and frequent times of confusion or feeling adrift as we attempt to navigate variabilities in the emotional terrain. So, when thinking about resilience in therapy, we must consider developing mental and emotional attitudes that will keep us engaged with our clients as they elaborate their experience, tolerate devastating emotions and trauma, accept ambiguity, make meaning of their symptoms and history, and think about how to effectively engage their reality.

This, as we all know, is no easy assignment. Staying in the chair, so to speak, being fully present physically, emotionally, and spiritually, is a task of endurance and commitment as we face the temptations of a wandering mind, defensive intellectualization, dissociation, or an overreliance on explaining, teaching, and encouragement—anything that allows us to not feel the devastating impact of our client's predicament. Further, an intimate connection to our client's pain activates our emotional vulnerability and suffering, threatening us with a resurgence of memories and relational confusions we thought we had reasonably harnessed. All of these factors exact an emotional toll, to say nothing of the looming shame and exposure that haunts us when our clients fail to get better, quit prematurely, attack us, diminish our skills, or simply refuse to participate in reasonable treatment interventions. Any combination of these feelings or self-states can leave us questioning our competence, ushering in shame or fears of inadequacy. Are we doing anything worthwhile?

Obviously, this rather sober portrayal does not capture all or even most of our clinical experience, but it does offer a glimpse into the challenges of our vocation, proving it is not for the faint of heart. Clinical work calls for strength of character and a *thick faith*.[8] In this context we appreciate Matthew Bates's (2017) depiction of faith in the Christian tradition as not being equivalent to believing, trusting, or feeling something is true or right. Rather, faith refers to an "embodied loyalty" (p. 5), a position of allegiance or fidelity to Christ. Eugene Peterson (1980), borrowing a phrase from Friedrich Nietzsche, says something similar when he talks about how Christians are formed through *a long obedience in the same direction*.[9]

In this light a resilient or thick spirituality is robust and able to maintain the hopeful longing for love, justice, freedom, and virtue despite threats to our sense of meaning and periods of unintelligible trauma. We are not suggesting that counselors and therapists deny or avoid their confusion and uncertainty, even about the reality of God in the world or their relationship to the divine. We are speaking to a hardiness in one's allegiance to God that can tolerate failure and uncertainty in clinical work and continue to pursue an elaboration of meaning and relational understanding. This will often entail reworking theological categories or tolerating the explanatory limits of one's own Christian tradition. It requires the capacity to mentalize our clients' experience of God as well, tuning into what God might be up to in their lives and the therapeutic relationship. Sustaining our capacity for vibrant relational connection while tolerating the complexity of clinical work calls for an

---

[8]We have used the term *thick* at different points in this book. Clifford Geertz (1973) is perhaps most closely associated with this term (although it did not originate with him), and our use of it follows his idea that a thick understanding goes beyond just describing human action or an individual's current thoughts and feelings. Rather, a thick description seriously considers the cultural context or historical setting of the person or community we are attempting to describe.

[9]Although not commonly noted in Christian circles, Nietzsche's original use of the phrase "a long obedience in the same direction" is not that different from what Peterson was intimating. Nietzsche, who coined the phrase in *Beyond Good and Evil*, originally published in 1886, was referring to the pursuit of something worth living for, something to which one may dedicate one's life.

internalization of God in a way that grounds us in the face of confusion, vulnerability, and diminishment.

What practices lead to a thick spirituality? In their essay on self-care of a relational psychoanalyst, authors Roy Barsness and Anita Sorenson (2018) highlight how the contemporary shift away from focusing on insight as the primary mechanism of therapeutic change to "the reworking of early trauma within the therapeutic dyad" (p. 302) places new strains and expectations on therapists and counselors. This is not unique to psychoanalytic theory and practice; the field of clinical mental health has increasingly become aware that the person of the therapist/counselor and the relationship that is formed with the client are essential factors influencing therapeutic progress and client growth (see Norcross & Lambert, 2019; Tishby & Wiseman, 2018). In other words, when it comes to our clients getting better, who we are in the room is just as, if not more, important as what we know. Accordingly, for those of us interested in clinically integrative practice, we can assume that our own relational spirituality, how it forms and is nurtured, will be very relevant to how our clients experience God and their own spirituality in the therapy relationship. We propose at least four critical dimensions to consider when developing a vibrant and resilient spirituality in clinical practice:

- spiritual practices that orient and ground us in the Spirit
- spiritual practices of remembrance
- spiritual practices that expand our emotional capacities, vitalize our self-experience, and hearten our tolerance for complexity, ambiguity, and uncertainty
- spiritual practices that connect us to a deep and sustaining relational community

Let's briefly consider each dimension separately, even though we know there will be many points of crossover as we discuss each area. Further, any examples we provide are for the purpose of stimulating your mind and heart to consider what might be effective methods that fit your circumstances and context.

Spiritual practices that orient and ground. In his fascinating book on the theology of an embodied God, Charles Halton (2021) discusses how one of the major challenges the ancient Israelites faced was maintaining a faithful belief in a disembodied God who refused to be represented by any graven image. Surrounded by competing religious traditions that could point to concrete images—Baal, Marduk, Asherah—Abraham and his descendants were called to trust and obey an intangible divine being who defied the limitations of ordinary sensory perception. While the Old Testament is replete with examples of how the Israelites struggled with and adapted to this conception of God, we face a similar and perhaps greater challenge. Remember how we discussed earlier in this chapter that we live in a buffered age, absent enchantment and easy attribution to the supernatural or mysterious. Much of our everyday experience tempts us to live as if God were irrelevant to our daily lives, suitable only for times of struggle, existential crisis, or moments of awe. Therefore, the question we are asking is: How do we maintain our orientation toward Christ, toward the reality of the spiritual life, toward the ground of our being (Tillich, 1952), in a manner that sustains our spiritual sensitivity in clinical work?[10] Maybe we can reflect now on this question. Just for a few moments, pause your reading and think with us about what you regularly do

---

[10]We realize that Tillich's phrase "ground of being" is entangled in his philosophical theology and that his specific meaning is somewhat unclear and has been batted about in various theological discussions. However, we find the phase useful and appreciate how Rennebohm and Thoburn (2021) discuss this concept, considering an incarnational psychotherapy in which divine essence is experienced as a "relational act of Christ among humanity" (p. 180).

in your life that orients you toward your identity as a Christian. Maybe jot down a few examples in the margin of this page.

As we think about this question, we come up with the many significant and insignificant behaviors or practices that orient us to the fact that we are Christian. Here we can think about the example of prayer, from the desperate times we've uttered, "Help me, Lord," to giving thanks before a meal, to praying for those we love, to praying for our clients. We think about our ritual of practicing Sabbath, participating in the Eucharist, giving money to charity, celebrating holy days, and attending to the rhythm of the church calendar. Earl frequently listens to a daily *lectio divina* podcast. Brad has engaged in spiritual direction and recently walked the Camino de Santiago. We both are drawn to books on theology, or, as this book attests, we write about our faith and work. We have colleagues who attend Mass more than once a week, pray the rosary, establish an icon corner that enhances or deepens personal prayer, and walk the stations of the cross every Good Friday. Many of us decorate our kitchens with kitschy Christian phrases, art, or designs. Both through direct recognition and unconscious association, we could probably all identify practices or rituals that we choose, sometimes automatically, sometimes begrudgingly, that reinforce the reality of our Christianity.

We also know that when we talk about orienting ourselves to our Christian tradition, we can get lost in troubling associations to the many spoken and unspoken obligations, expectations, or commands several of us received from others about how to be a good Christian. Did you pray today? Did you do your devotions? Are you reciting the Lord's Prayer? Did you attend small group or midweek Mass in addition to Sunday? Are you using your gifts for God by serving in church? Have you committed this Scripture passage to memory? Did you witness today? Did you go to confession? Do you believe the right theology? Do you believe it hard enough?

In too many cases these messages were communicated in a heavy-handed manner or with notes of disapproval, condemnation, or shame for those who didn't fall in line. In some egregious situations we have seen the spiritual practice itself become an activator for traumatic self-states, dissociation, or painful memories. As a result, we sometimes must get distance from the rituals of our past and forge new ones, or in some cases change our tradition altogether.

In sharp contrast to obligation and expectation, we believe the most beneficial posture to assume when orienting and grounding ourselves to the reality of Christ is a nonanxious attitude of freedom to participate in the divine invitation to a life of peace, hope, and love. In this light, we look at the practices of the faith not as *shoulds* or *oughts* but as methods to embrace in our own unique way as we pursue depth and growth in our Christian life. This does not mean that practices that ground and orient us will always be easy or light; some may take struggle, effort, and determination (Willard, 2006). But we should diligently try to evacuate any thought that these practices earn us a better standing with Christ. Rather, these are *ways of being* that Jesus says will help us be closer to him.

For example, if we think about some of the classic spiritual disciplines—solitude, fasting, generosity, worship, fellowship, confession, simplicity—we know that each of these binds us to the telos of God's love. They anchor us in a way of being in the world that directly influences the way we experience ourselves and our clinical work. In addition, contemplative practices such as *lectio divina*, the Examen, prayers of recollection, or Ignatian exercises serve to clear our minds and reenchant us with the Spirit. Beck (2021) encourages these spiritual practices and the immersion of ourselves into tangible experiences of our tradition—sights, sounds, and tastes—anything that fights against the insidious "slow death of God" (p. 22) brought on by our modern life.

Spiritual practices of remembrance. More than once, early in his discoveries regarding the human mind, Freud acknowledged that his talking cure—psychoanalysis—was essentially a cure through love (Haynal & Falzeder, 1991; McGuire, 1974). What's fascinating about these statements, made both in letters and in early meetings of the Vienna Psychoanalytic Society, is the almost complete absence of acknowledgment about this critical dimension of therapeutic work in the development of psychoanalytic theory and clinical practice over the next century.[11] Moving away from psychoanalytic theory into other theoretical models, we find an equal if not larger vacancy regarding any discussion of love as a critical element in therapeutic change. In general, most psychological theories conceptualize the therapeutic relationship as an alliance, where cooperative rapport is seen as a necessary element for change. Love for clients is generally not discussed for various reasons such as professionalism, anxieties about close associations to erotic love, and a variety of countertransference activations. Whatever the reason, thinking about love for our clients, and more specifically the therapeutic action of love, is somehow too close, too intimate, threatening our field's reliance on objective knowledge and dispassionate care. As Christians, we often think we are better at talking about love, that we easily say, "Of course, love cures; the love of God is what heals the world." Perhaps, but what are we really talking about? Is the shadow side of this sentiment something like, "I'm glad God loves my client, because I'm not so sure I do"?

---

[11]There are exceptions to this statement, of course, the most notable possibly Ian Suttie's (1988) *The Origins of Love and Hate* and more recently Marie Hoffman's (2011) *Toward Mutual Recognition*.

Part of our reason for talking about love is how easy it is for us to forget, even as Christians, what is at the essence of what we do as integrative clinicians. While theories and therapeutic methods can certainly emerge from a loving desire to promote healing and growth, too often we lose contact with the experience of love that grounds our efforts. Our colleague Roy Barsness (2018), in a fascinating qualitative study of senior psychoanalysts/therapists, asked each participant about their approach to clinical work and what they thought worked with their clients. Roy's findings provide support for and extensively elaborate Freud's initial impulse. Using a grounded theory analysis, Barsness identified seven competencies of an effective relational therapist, including therapeutic intent, deep listening, and courageous speech. After teasing out all the factors, Barsness concluded that these seven therapeutic elements were best captured in an overarching relational stance of love. Clearly, we are not talking about love as a sentimentality or attraction—we are speaking about a thick relational connection and steadfast, loving presence that is able to persevere through the ups and downs of clinical work for the betterment of the client.

Just like we need reminding about the essence of love that works its way through our clinical work, we are in constant need of recollecting the love of God for us. While it can be centering and vitalizing to participate in Christian rituals for remembering the love of God—think about the Eucharist, Christmas, or Easter celebrations—we find that clinical work often challenges our private experience of feeling loved and secure in our sense of self. Recall our previous discussion about the ways in which clinical work can challenge our competency, activate old traumas and relational wounds, leave us grasping for something intelligent to say or exhausted in the face of client resistance and attack. During these times our self-esteem takes a beating, leaving us with feelings of isolation, shame, and helplessness. Here we want to ask how you might find your way back to remembering who God is and how God sees you and your work. Through her *Prayer of Recollection*, Teresa of Ávila provided one path as she encouraged us to invite Jesus into the intimate spaces of our confusion, fatigue, and pain.[12] Imagining his presence, we are reminded of who Christ is, his love for us, and begin to recollect the fragmented parts of ourselves. Spiritual practices of recollecting and remembering highlight the inescapable nature of God's love. There is no place we can go where love doesn't follow.

Spiritual practices that expand our emotional capacities. Buechler (2008) suggests that one of the most important emotional capacities for a therapist or counselor is the "capacity for comfort in the unfinished" (p. 234). Because much of our work involves helping people live and prosper within the context of their messy lives, very rarely are problems or symptoms totally resolved. Steven Cooper (2016) sees tolerating these limits and incompleteness as the "melancholic errand" (p. 46) of our work. This does not mean we don't have success and that clients don't get better. Rather, ours is a work of "struggling with the tension between wanting the client to develop and grow as much as possible, and the capacity to understand the intrinsic incompleteness of his or her life" (p. 7). To our ears this sounds like deep wisdom and helps speak to the pervasive ambiguity and complications we find in working with people who have suffered. Unwittingly, these authors are speaking to a Christian theological assumption of the *already and the not yet*. This paradox, fundamental to the Christian sensibility toward ethics, is on the one hand an orientation to participate in partnership with God to

---

[12]There are numerous online examples of this prayer as well as instructions for participation. *St. Theresa's Own Words* is a book with instructions on the prayer of recollection that can be found in numerous forms of publication.

achieve healing and liberation in the life of our clients now. On the other hand, we realize that the fulfillment of a pervasive "*commonwealth of love and justice*" (Fowler, 2000, p. 68, italics original) is partial, progressive, and developmental—requiring a deep hope and persistence in our expression of the Christian vocation.

In addition to patience and comfort with imperfect endings, our work requires a posture of integrative complexity (Békés & Suedfeld, 2019). One need only sit in a few sessions to realize that a capacity to hold in mind multiple perspectives, dimensions, or meanings of our clients and their lives is no easy task and often takes consistent practice, consultation, and/or supervision. In addition, the information we hold about and for our clients is not abstract data. It is emotionally evocative and often contradictory or only partially revealed. It is well known that mental health symptoms and relational problems have no single cause. They are overdetermined, and although it might be clinically expedient, pragmatic, or emotionally calming to pare down the many factors involved, we cannot escape our own need to consider the complexity of our clients' context so that we may provide the best care possible. Moreover, our clients often make choices in their life, relational or otherwise, that might conflict with our values. Our beliefs and preferences are challenged, and the choices of those we work with can feel strange, unusual, or even immoral. Beyond opening ourselves to the differentness and diversity of our clients' identities and pasts, how do we process the different perceptions, interpretations, and conclusions of our clients in a posture of steadfast love?

Given these three dimensions of our work—incompleteness, complexity, and values conflict—we wonder what additional spiritual practices might help us tolerate uncertainty, complexity, and the oft incomplete nature of our work. Two suggestions come to mind. First, for hundreds of years Christians of all traditions have been engaged in some form of the daily Examen. With roots in the Ignatian spiritual tradition, the daily Examen is a process of prayerful reflection about one's thoughts and actions during the day. While there are many variations, the general thrust of the exercise is to consider what is happening or what has happened in our day and consider/listen to how the Spirit may be desiring to lead or correct us in our daily walk. An Examen process for clinically integrative practice may look a little different, and below we have adapted a process suggested by Father Dennis Hamm (1994) in his work *Rummaging for God*.

With an attitude of prayerful reflection in the middle or end of the day:

1. Ask God for light so that you may look at your clinical experience with clients though God's eyes, not just your own.
2. Give thanks to God for the day and your ability to work with clients.
3. Rummage around in your memories of the day, reflecting on the work with clients that has just finished. Pay attention to your emotional reactions and developing associations. As the mix of positive and negative feelings emerges, attend to the situations from which they developed.
4. Choose one or two emotional states that seem to dominate and pray from inside this emotion, recognizing that the strength of emotion suggests something important is going on. The prayer does not have to be formal; rather, allow yourself to spontaneously seek God in the feeling. Perhaps you are pleading to God for clarity and understanding about what to do or say in the next session. Maybe you praise God for movement, growth, or change. This might also be the place for confession and contrition.

5. Close your Examen with an eye toward tomorrow, asking God for understanding, courage, and however else you might need the Spirit in the day and week ahead.

The process is not meant to be burdensome but an invitation free of condemnation or shame. In the context of clinical practice, we can reflect on how God might be welcoming us to consider where he is in our work and the lives of our clients.

A second spiritual practice may sound a bit out of the ordinary, but we follow a cue from C. Steven Evans (1989) when he suggests that psychologists and counselors should broaden their exposure to different ways of thinking about the world by reading philosophy.[13] While this is true, we also want to encourage exposure to the wide divergence of thought that exists in all the arts and humanities. Several authors have written about how literature and the arts open up space for thinking about the human condition and clinical work, particularly because good poetry, art, and literature can bypass conscious intellectual critique and move directly to our feelings (e.g., Charles, 2015; Griffin, 2016). Think about the way film and theater capture us at a visceral level. Further, and this may seem like a rather elementary suggestion, it is essential to challenge our tendency to live in an echo chamber of our own thinking and ways of being, to expose ourselves to the diversity of thought and experience in the world, including what makes us uncomfortable. On these edges of growth, we see other ways of being human that are just as valid as our own. But this is not enough; we find that education in crosscultural issues or diversity and inclusion is inadequate if this training does not challenge us at an emotional/relational level.

---

[13]We also advocate that the integrative clinician continue to read theology for its own sake, not just integrative literature. Furthermore, this theology should be, at least at times, outside your own tradition or written by a theologian different from you.

Meeting the challenge to embrace complexity and diversity requires curiosity, empathy, and humility. The self-emptying, kenotic walk of humility in the face of difference allows for the possibility of connectedness. As we become curious about the other with an attitude of *steadfast love*, the possibility for surrender emerges. Here we are talking about Emmanuel Ghent's (1990) notion of surrender (over against submission, compliance to a more powerful or dominant other). Surrender, the nonconscious releasing of our own priority with the simultaneous capacity to hold ourselves in a nonanxious presence in the service of relational engagement—this is the kenotic model that allows for entrance into the feared places difference can evoke.

Spiritual practices that connect us to a deep and sustaining relational community. Our final area of spirituality involves the purposeful pursuit of a relational community that fosters our growth, witnesses our struggles, and celebrates our flourishing. In a previous work Brad (Brown & Strawn, 2012) wrote about the importance of an embodied experience within a church community to combat our current tendency to see spirituality as "individual, private, and inner," almost to the exclusion of participatory, embodied spirituality that is interested in forming a character that "has a greater capacity for hospitality, love, and care for others" (p. 109). Although we believe in the importance of the church, even with all its knots and imperfections, we are more concerned with finding and developing a sustainable Christian community that allows us to rub shoulders with other believers as we *slouch* toward change and growth. To grow and change, we need people, and we need people who are different from us and imperfect in their uniqueness to help us become more adaptable, flexible, accepting, and caring. We are natural-born imitators, and Christian community offers unique conscious and unconscious opportunities for imitative spiritual formational practices.

In addition to a well-functioning Christian community, we also need a professional community that knows the challenges of clinical work and how this type of work affects us emotionally and relationally over the long term. Practically speaking, this may be a professional organization, coworkers, or a reading/consultation group. Whatever the form, we believe there should be some outlet for frank conversation, emotional support, truth telling, and laughter. In these spaces we want to invite people who are different from us, but we also want spaces of identification and sameness, to look in the eyes of an intimate colleague who just gets us.

Last, and this will vary from person to person, we find that sustaining ourselves as integrative clinicians requires that we engage in community with those who are not associated with our profession at all. Here we often find a corrective to our professional hubris and encounter the many varieties of human experience and the *therapies* that a full engagement in life provides. As we participate in life with others, the joys and challenges, the work and the play, we come to embrace the range of ways people live effective and meaningful lives that have very little to do with formal clinical treatment. Indeed, this is refreshing and helps us to contextualize our own work within the broader healing power of God's creation.

SUMMARY AND QUESTIONS FOR CONSIDERATION

We hope reading this chapter has left you with a sense of freedom and curiosity regarding how you might develop spiritual and relational practices that sustain you in this *impossible profession*. When Freud (1937) used this descriptor, he was referencing the uncertainty, doubt, and less than fully satisfying results therapy often gives us. A similar sentiment is expressed by Steven Garber

(2014), suggesting that the pursuit of any vocation must face the limitations brought on by working with real people in real circumstances. In his words, "learning to live proximately" (p. 195) means that we must come to peace with the realization that more could always be done, that we are always operating within our current time, and that we are necessarily constrained by the limits of our knowledge, our skill, and the givens of a world we must all inhabit. Yet Garber, while calling for a courageous and engaged posture in the face of these realities, also reminds us that the Christion *vision of vocation*

> incarnates this conviction, telling the story of the Word becoming flesh, and of words becoming flesh in and through our vocation. This vision calls us to know and to care about what we know; in fact to love what we know. . . . We will never do that perfectly, only proximately, at our very best. But in this now-but-not-yet moment in history, that is enough. (p. 224)

Here we see Garber pulling from a deep Christian ethic that allows us to operate with hope in the face of a profession that often confronts us with the brokenness and heartache of our fallen world. This hope, however, requires nourishment through intentional practices that keep us continually expectant of God's work in our work. As you think about constructing a resilient pursuit of clinically integrative practice, perhaps the following questions will aid in the pursuit and maintenance of this mindset:

- As you think about your current spiritual and religious life, what practices do you currently engage in that keep you grounded and oriented to a Christian ethic in your work?
- In what way does your professional life and work interrupt or distract you from thinking integratively? What activities, personal or communal, do you use to recollect the love of God in your life and work?

- How do you experience the Spirit's movement in your work? In what way might your emotional awareness be enhanced by considering the presence of the Spirit's work in therapeutic relationships.

- How does your communal life enhance your hope and faith? In what ways, if any, does your current community detract from your ability to consider God's work in your work?

While these questions are meant to stimulate your thinking, we think it is important to remember that the Christian life is one of invitation, not coercion or manipulation. In other words, we offer this chapter from a position of welcoming hospitality as you consider exploring your spiritual life and building practices of resilience.

(A KIND OF) CONCLUSION

We have now reached the end of this dialogue. As we said in the introduction, we hoped that this book would be a kind of conversation—a conversation based on the possibility that if we held our perspectives loosely enough, we would have a dialogue, as opposed to a debate, and in that vulnerability both parties might be changed. Another way to say this, consistent with our approach, is that something new might emerge.

We are happy to share with you that from our end, writing this book has facilitated the emergence of new thoughts, feelings, and experiences for the two of us authors. It has been born of our discussions with each other, our personal and professional histories, and from our real-time conversations with students and colleagues. It has pushed us to articulate ideas we have only vaguely sensed. It has compelled us to strive for clarity while holding convictions loosely enough that you the reader may push back, wrestle with, and even rework our ideas. Writing the book has genuinely aided us to move much of our implicit experience to explicit expression. For us this has been worth the journey, and we want to thank you for sharing your time as you have considered our mindsets.

Another powerful reason we have written this book is because after sixty-some cumulative years of clinical work, we still love it! As Sandra Buechler (2012) says, we are *still practicing*. We are still fascinated by the work, still challenged, still frustrated (at times), still dumbfounded, still honored, and still resilient. While both of us wear several vocational hats (professor, researcher, pastor, family member, etc.), we can't imagine giving up this clinical integrative work. The world desperately needs passionate clinical integrative practitioners, and we hope and pray that after thirty years of practicing you too will maintain your passion, resilience, and well-being in the field.

As our conversation comes to a close, we want to ask you a few questions. As you have been reading, what has emerged for you? What have you found yourself both thinking and feeling? Are there aspects of the domains or mindset that have particularly affected you? What clinical situations and memories have come to mind? In a sense, we want to invite you to consider a kind of *personal-developmental integrative treatment plan*—not for your clients but for yourself.

When you think of the five domains that matter—hermeneutics, tradition, ethics, self-development, and resilience—consider the following:

1. Are there particular domains in which you want to continue to develop?
2. Have the domains caused you to consider letting go of something (e.g., what counts as integration) or to lessen your emphasis (e.g., what makes something Christian)?
3. What from the book doesn't fit for you?
4. Where do you need to push back or rearrange to possibly fit your religious tradition, culture, social location, and so on?
5. What will you do in response to the above questions? In other words, what settings will be necessary for you, and what kind of practices will you need to engage in, to continue your integrative development?

(A Kind of) Conclusion

This book has been primarily organized around the idea that integrative moments in clinical work emerge from the complex dynamic system, that is, the clinical moment itself. Again, this suggests we can't predict, control, or master integration. We can't define integration or even say what makes it Christian—if that is your goal. And while this might create some anxiety, we have suggested that there are settings, practices, and a kind of mindset that we believe create the needed complexity that not only allows for the possibility of emergence but also facilitates our capacity to stay attuned to what God is up to in the clinical moment.

What this means is that this book is only the beginning of an ongoing journey of emergence for you. We hope that you will keep emerging as a clinical integrative practitioner. For example, we pray you won't think, feel, and perceive in ten years what you do today. Not only is this change good for you and for your clients, but we also believe it is evidence of the Spirit's ongoing work in your vocational calling. So, while we can't control emergence, we do believe we can engage in these settings and practices and hold the mindsets (i.e., domains that matter in integration) that can make all the difference. We hope you embrace an ongoing dialogue, comfortable and uncomfortable emergence, and an ever-growing capacity to always see what God is up to.

REFERENCES

Abu-Raiya, H. (2015). Working with religious Muslim clients: A dynamic, Qur'anic-based model of psychotherapy. *Spirituality in Clinical Practice, 2*(2), 120-33.

Adams, J. E. (1970). *Competent to counsel*. Baker.

Allison, E., & Fonagy, P. (2016). When is truth relevant? *The Psychoanalytic Quarterly, 85*(2), 275-303.

Aten, J. D., McMinn, M. R., & Worthington, E. L. (Eds.). (2011). *Spiritually oriented interventions for counseling and psychotherapy*. American Psychological Association.

Atwood, G. E., & Stolorow, R. D. (1993). *Faces in a cloud: Intersubjectivity in personality theory*. Jason Aronson.

Balswick, J. O., King, P. E., & Reimer, K. S. (2016). *The reciprocating self: Human development in theological perspective* (2nd ed.). InterVarsity Press.

Barsness, R. E. (Ed.). (2018). *Core competencies of relational psychoanalysis: A guide to practice, study, and research*. Routledge.

Barsness, R. E., & Sorenson, A. L. (2018). Staying connected when things fall apart: The personal and professional life of the analyst. In R. E. Barsness (Ed.), *Core competencies of relational psychoanalysis: A guide to practice, study, and research* (pp. 302-17). Routledge.

Barsness, R. E., & Strawn, B. D. (2018). Relational psychoanalytic ethics, professional, personal, theoretical, and communal. In R. E. Barsness (Ed.), *Core competencies of relational psychoanalysis: A guide to practice, study, and research* (pp. 221-40). Routledge.

Bates, M. W. (2017). *Salvation by allegiance alone: Rethinking faith, works, and the gospel of Jesus the king*. Baker Academic.

Beck, R. (2021). *Hunting magic eels: Recovering an enchanted faith in a skeptical age*. Broadleaf Books.

Békés, V., & Suedfeld, P. (2019). Integrative complexity. In V. Zeigler-Hill & T. K. Shackelford (Eds.), *Encyclopedia of personality and individual differences* (pp. 1-5). Springer.

Bellah, R. N., Madsen, R., Sullivan, W., Swidler, A., & Tipton, S. M. (1985). *Habits of the heart: Individualism and commitment in American life*. University of California Press.

Benjamin, J. A. (2018). *Beyond doer and done to: Recognition theory, intersubjectivity and the third*. Routledge.
Benner, D. G. (1988). *Psychotherapy and the spiritual quest*. Baker.
Benner, D. G. (2011). *Soulful spirituality: Becoming fully alive and deeply human*. Brazos.
Bland, C. S., Brue, J. S., White, J., & Sartor, D. (2018, April). *Beyond bracketing: Exploring alternative paradigms in value conflicts* [Presentation]. Christian Association for Psychological Studies, Norfolk, VA.
Bland, E. D., & Strawn, B. D. (Eds.). (2014). *Christianity and psychoanalysis: A new conversation*. IVP Academic.
Bland, E. D., & Strawn, B. D. (2024). Situating John Carter within a brief history of the integration of psychology and theology. *Journal of Psychology and Christianity, 43*(1), 7-14.
Boston Process of Change Study Group. (2010). *Change in psychotherapy: A unifying paradigm*. Norton.
Brenner, C. (1974). *An elementary textbook of psychoanalysis* (Rev. ed.). Knopf.
Brown, W. S. (2004). Resonance: A model for relating science, psychology, and faith. *Journal of Psychology and Christianity, 23*, 110-20.
Brown, W. S., & Strawn, B. D. (2012). *The physical nature of Christian life: Neuroscience, psychology, and the church*. Cambridge University Press.
Browning, D. S., & Cooper, T. D. (2004). *Religious thought and the modern psychologies* (2nd ed.). Fortress.
Buechler, S. (2008). *Making a difference in patients' lives: Emotional experience in the therapeutic setting*. Routledge.
Buechler, S. (2012). *Still practicing: The heartaches and joys of a clinical career*. Routledge.
Carpenter, A. (2020). *Responsive becoming: Moral formation in theological, evolutionary, and developmental perspective*. T&T Clark.
Carter, J. D., & Narramore, B. (1979). *The integration of psychology and theology: An introduction*. Zondervan.
Cates, L. B. (2014). Insidious emotional trauma: The body remembers . . . *International Journal of Psychoanalytic Self Psychology, 9*, 35-53.
Charles, M. (2015). *Psychoanalysis and literature: The stories we live*. Rowman & Littlefield.
Coe, J. H., & Hall, T. W. (2010). *Psychology in the Spirit: Contours of a transformational psychology*. IVP Academic.
Collicutt, J. (2015). *The psychology of Christian character formation*. SCM Press.
Comas-Diaz, L., & Rivera, E. T. (2020). (Eds.). *Liberation psychology: Theory, method, practice, and social justice*. American Psychological Association.
Cone, J. (2011). *The cross and the lynching tree*. Orbis Books.
Cone, J. H. (1997). *God of the oppressed* (Rev. ed.). Orbis Books.

Cooper, S. H. (2016). *The analyst's experience of the depressive position: The melancholic errand of psychoanalysis*. Routledge.

Crisp, T. M., Porter, S. L., & Ten Elshof, G. A. (Eds.). (2019). *Psychology and spiritual formation in dialogue: Moral and spiritual change in Christian perspective*. IVP Academic.

Cushman, P. (1995). *Constructing self, constructing America: A cultural history of psychotherapy*. Da Capo.

Cushman, P. (2020). Two worlds or one? Politics inside and outside the consulting room. *Psychoanalysis, Self and Context, 15*(3), 218-26.

Doherty, W. J. (1995). *Soul searching: Why psychotherapy must promote moral responsibility*. Basic Books.

Dowling, E. M., & Scarlett, W. G. (Eds.). (2006). *Encyclopedia of religious and spiritual development*. Sage.

Du Bois, W. E. B. (1903). *The souls of Black folk: Essays and sketches*. A. C. McClurg.

Dueck, A. (2002). Babel, Esperanto, shibboleths, and Pentecost: Can we talk? *Journal of Psychology and Christianity, 21*(1), 72-80.

Dueck, A., & Reimer, K. (2009). *A peaceable psychology: Christian therapy in a world of many cultures*. Brazos.

Dwiwardani, C., & Whitney, W. B. (2022). The cycle of cultural integration: Toward hermeneutical justice in the integration of psychology and theology. *Journal of Psychology and Theology, 52*(2), 237-51.

Entwistle, D. N. (2021). *Integrative approaches to psychology and Christianity: An introduction to worldview issues, philosophical foundations, and models of integration* (4th ed.). Cascade Books.

Evans, C. S. (1989). *Wisdom and humanness in psychology: Prospects for a Christian approach*. Baker Book House.

Faw, H. W. (1998). Wilderness wanderings and promised integration: The quest for clarity. *Journal of Psychology & Theology, 26*(2), 147-58.

Fisher, L. (2021). *Diversity in clinical practice: A practical & shame-free guide to reducing cultural offenses and repairing cross-cultural relationships*. PESI.

Flemming, D. (2005). *Contextualization in the New Testament: Patterns for theology and mission*. IVP Academic.

Fonagy, P., Gergely, G., Jurist, E., & Target, M. (2004). *Affect regulation, mentalization, and the development of the self*. Other Press.

Fors, M. (2018). *A grammar of power in psychotherapy: Exploring the dynamics of privilege*. American Psychological Association.

Fowler, J. W. (2000). *Becoming adult, becoming Christian: Adult development and Christian faith*. Jossey-Bass.

Freud, S. (1937). Analysis terminable and interminable. *The International Journal of Psychoanalysis, 18*(4), 373-405.

Fromm, E. (1950). *Psychotherapy and religion (The Terry lectures)*. Yale University Press.

Gadamer, H.-G. (1975). *Truth and method*. Continuum.
Garber, S. (2014). *Visions of vocation: Common grace for the common good*. InterVarsity Press.
Geertz, C. (1973). *The interpretation of cultures: Selected essays*. Basic Books.
Ghent, E. (1990). Masochism, submission, surrender—Masochism as a perversion of surrender. *Contemporary Psychoanalysis, 26*, 108-36.
Greggo, S. P., & Sisemore, T. A. (Eds.). (2012). *Counseling and Christianity: Five approaches*. IVP Academic.
Grenz, S. J. (2001). *The social God and the relational self: A trinitarian theology of the imago Dei*. Westminster John Knox.
Grenz, S. J., & Olson, R. E. (1992). *Twentieth-century theology: God and the world in a transitional age*. InterVarsity Press.
Griffin, F. L. (2016). *Creative listening and the psychoanalytic process*. Routledge.
Griffith, J. L., & Griffith, M. E. (2002). *Encountering the sacred in psychotherapy: How to talk to people about their spiritual lives*. Guilford.
Hall, T. W., & Hall, M. E. L. (2021). *Relational spirituality: A psychological-theological paradigm for transformation*. InterVarsity Press.
Halton, C. (2021). *A human-shaped God: Theology of an embodied God*. Westminster John Knox.
Hamm, D. (1994). Rummaging for God: Praying backwards through your day. *America*, 22-23.
Hathaway, W. L. (2002). Integration as interpretation: A hermeneutical-realist view. *Journal of Psychology and Christianity, 21*(3), 205-18.
Hathaway, W. L. (2011). Ethical guidelines for using spiritually oriented interventions. In M. Leach, M. McMinn, & E. Worthington (Eds.), *Spiritually oriented interventions for counseling and psychotherapy* (pp. 65-81). American Psychological Association.
Hathaway, W. L., & Yarhouse, M. A. (2021). *The integration of psychology and Christianity: A domain-based approach*. IVP Academic.
Haugen, H. M. (2018). It is time for a general comment on children's spiritual development. *International Journal of Children's Spirituality, 3*, 306-22.
Haynal, A., & Falzeder, E. (1991). Healing through love? *Free Associations, 2*(1), 1-20.
Hays, R. B. (2020). *Reading with the grain of Scripture*. Eerdmans.
Hazanov, V. (2019). *The fear of doing nothing: Notes of a young therapist*. Sphinx Books.
Hoard, P., & Bland, E. D. (2023). "How am I responsible?": Evangelical white rage and moral injury in the interpassive perpetration of white-body supremacy. *Psychoanalytic Dialogues, 33*(5), 653-70.
Hoffman, M. T. (2011). *Toward mutual recognition: Relational psychoanalysis and the Christian narrative*. Routledge.
Hoffman, M. T. (2016). *When the roll is called: Trauma and the soul of American evangelicalism*. Cascade Books.

James, W. (1994). *The varieties of religious experience*. Random House.
Jeeves, M. A., & Ludwig, T. E. (2018). *Psychological science and Christian faith: Insights and enrichments from constructive dialogue*. Templeton.
Johnson, E. L. (2007). *Foundations for soul care: A Christian psychology proposal*. IVP Academic.
Johnson, E. L. (Ed.). (2010). *Psychology and Christianity: Five views* (2nd ed.). InterVarsity Press.
Johnson, E. L., & Jones, S. L. (Eds.). (2000). *Psychology and Christianity: Four views*. InterVarsity Press.
Jones, S. L. (Ed.). (1986). *Psychology and the Christian faith: An introductory reader*. Baker.
Jones, S. L. (1994). A constructive relationship for religion with the science and profession of psychology: Perhaps the boldest model yet. *American Psychologist, 49*(3), 184-99.
Joshi, K. Y. (2020). *White Christian privilege: The illusion of religious equality in America*. New York University Press.
Knabb, J., Johnson, E., & Garzon, F. (2020). Introduction to the special issue: Meditation, prayer, and contemplation in the Christian tradition: Towards the operationalization and clinical application of Christian practices in psychotherapy and counseling. *Journal of Psychology and Christianity, 39*(1), 5-11.
Layton, L. (2004). A fork in the royal road: On "defining" the unconscious and its stakes for social theory. *Psychoanalysis, Culture & Society, 9*, 33-51.
Leclerc, D., & Maddix, M. A. (2011). *Spiritual formation: A Wesleyan paradigm*. Beacon Hill
MacIntyre, A. (1984). *After virtue: A study in moral theory* (2nd ed.). University of Notre Dame Press.
Malony, H. N., & Vande Kemp, H. (1995). *Psychology and the cross: The early history of Fuller Seminary's School of Psychology*. Fuller Seminary Press.
McGuire, W. (Ed.). (1974). *The Freud/Jung letters: The correspondence between Sigmund Freud and C. G. Jung*. Princeton University Press.
McLaughlin, P. T., & McMinn, M. R. (2022). *A time for wisdom: Knowledge, detachment, tranquility, transcendence*. Templeton.
McMinn, M. R., & Campbell, C. D. (2007). *Integrative psychotherapy: Toward a comprehensive Christian approach*. IVP Academic.
McNeil, J. D. (2005). Unequally yoked?: The role of culture in the relationship between theology and psychology. In A. Dueck & C. Lee (Eds.), *Why psychology needs theology: A radical-reformation perspective* (pp. 140-62). Eerdmans.
McNeil, J. D. (2010). Reluctant integration. In G. Moriarty (Ed.), *Integrating faith and psychology: Twelve psychologists tell their story* (pp. 188-208). InterVarsity Press.
Milner, M. (2011). *A life of one's own*. Routledge.
Moon, G. (1997). *Homesick for Eden: A soul's journey to joy*. Servant Publications.

Murphy, N. (1996). *Beyond liberalism and fundamentalism: How modern and postmodern philosophy set the theological agenda*. Trinity Press International.

Neff, M. A., & McMinn, M. R. (2020). *Embodying integration: A fresh look at Christianity in the therapy room*. IVP Academic.

Norcross, J. C., Beutler, L. E., & Levant, R. F. (Eds.). (2006). *Evidence-based practices in mental health: Debate and dialogue on the fundamental questions*. American Psychological Association.

Norcross, J. C., & Lambert, M. J. (Eds.). (2019). *Psychotherapy relationships that work: Evidence-based contributions* (3rd ed., Vol. 1). Oxford University Press.

Olthuis, J. H. (2001). *The beautiful risk: A new psychology of loving and being loved*. Zondervan.

Orange, D. M. (1995). *Emotional understanding: Studies in psychoanalytic epistemology*. Guilford.

Orange, D. M. (2016). *Nourishing the inner life of clinicians and humanitarians*. Routledge.

Pargament, K. I. (2011). *Spiritually integrated psychotherapy: Understanding and addressing the sacred*. Guilford.

Pargament, K. I., & Exline, J. J. (2022). *Working with spiritual struggles in psychotherapy: From research to practice*. Guilford.

Peterson, E. H. (1980). *A long obedience in the same direction: Discipleship in an instant society*. InterVarsity Press.

Peterson, E. H. (2002). *The message*. NavPress.

Polanyi, M. (1958). *Personal knowledge: Towards a post-critical philosophy*. University of Chicago Press.

Powlison, D. (2010). A biblical counseling view. In E. L. Johnson (Ed.), *Psychology and Christianity: Five views* (2nd ed., pp. 245-73). IVP Academic.

Reed, L. F. (2024). Integrating psychological and theological perspectives on multiculturalism, social justice, and peace. *Journal of Psychology & Theology, 52*(2), 131-40.

Rennebohm, S. B., & Thoburn, J. (2021). Incarnational psychotherapy: Christ as the ground of being for integrating psychology and theology. *Pastoral Psychology, 70*, 179-90.

Richardson, F. C., Fowers, B. J., & Guignon, C. B. (1999). *Re-envisioning psychology: Moral dimensions of theory and practice*. Jossey-Bass.

Sandage, S. J., & Brown, J. K. (2018). *Relational integration of psychology and Christian theology: Theory, research, and practice*. Routledge.

Sandage, S. J., & Strawn, B. D. (Eds.). (2022). *Spiritual diversity in psychotherapy: Engaging the sacred in clinical practice*. American Psychological Association.

Sarnat, J. E. (2019). What's new in parallel process? The evolution of supervision's signature phenomenon. *The American Journal of Psychoanalysis, 79*, 304-28.

Shults, F. L., & Sandage, S. J. (2006). *Transforming spirituality: Integrating theology and psychology*. Baker Academic.

Smith, C., & Denton, M. L. (2009). *Soul searching: The religious and spiritual lives of American teenagers*. Oxford University Press.

Smith, J. K. A. (2009). *Desiring the kingdom: Worship, worldview, and cultural formation*. Baker Academic.

Smith, J. K. A. (2016). *You are what you love: The spiritual power of habit*. Brazos.

Sorenson, R. L. (2004). *Minding spirituality*. The Analytic Press.

Sperry, L. (2012). *Spirituality in clinical practice: Theory and practice of spiritually-oriented psychotherapy*. (2nd ed.). Routledge.

Steere, D. A. (1997). *Spiritual presence in psychotherapy: A guide for caregivers*. Brunner Mazel.

Stern, D. B. (2017). Interpersonal psychoanalysis: History and current status. *Contemporary Psychoanalysis, 53*(1), 69-94.

Stern, D. N. (1985). *The interpersonal world of the infant: A view from psychoanalysis and development*. Basic Books.

Stern, D. N. (2004). *The present moment in psychotherapy and everyday life*. Norton.

Stolorow, R. D. (2013). Intersubjective-systems theory: A phenomenological-contextualist psychoanalytic perspective. *Psychoanalytic Dialogues, 23*, 383-89.

Stolorow, R. D., & Atwood, G. E. (1992). *Contexts of being: The intersubjective foundations of psychological life*. Analytic.

Strawn, B. D. (2016). Integration: What with what and with whom? *Fuller Magazine, 5*, 39-43.

Strawn, B. D., & Bland, E. D. (2018). Clinical integration: A case study approach [Special issue]. *Journal of Psychology and Theology, 46*(2).

Strawn, B. D., Bland, E. D., & Flores, P. S. (2018). Learning clinical integration: A case study approach. *Journal of Psychology & Theology, 46*(2), 85-97.

Strawn, B. D., & Brown, W. S. (2020). *Enhancing the Christian life: How extended cognition augments religious community*. IVP Academic.

Strawn, B. D., Wright, R. W., & Jones, P. (2014). Tradition-based integration: Illuminating the stories and practices that shape our integrative imagination. *Journal of Psychology and Christianity, 33*(4), 300-310.

Sussman, M. B. (2007). *A curious calling: Unconscious motivations for practicing psychotherapy* (2nd ed.). Jason Aronson.

Suttie, I. D. (1988). *The origins of love and hate*. Free Association Books.

Tan, S.-Y. (1996). Religion in clinical practice: Implicit and explicit integration. In E. P. Shafranske (Ed.), *Religion and the clinical practice of psychology* (pp. 365-87). American Psychological Association.

Taylor, C. (2003). *Modern social imaginaries*. Duke University Press.

Taylor, C. (2007). *A secular age*. Belknap Press.

Taylor, C. (2011). *Dilemmas and connections: Selected essays*. Belknap Press.

Thelen, E., & Smith, L. B. (1994). *A dynamic systems approach to the development of cognition and action*. MIT Press.

Tillich, P. (1952). *The courage to be*. Yale University Press.

Tishby, O., & Wiseman, H. (2018). *Developing the therapeutic relationship: Integrating case studies, research, and practice*. American Psychological Association.

Tronick, E. (2007). *Neurobehavioral and social emotional development*. W. W. Norton.

Tronick, E. (2022). Trauma never occurs only once: Being traumatized by a slap is like making meaning of the game of peek-a-boo. *Psychoanalytic Dialogues, 32*(6), 661-73.

Tronick, E., & Beeghly, M. (2011). Meaning making and infant mental health. *American Psychologist, 66*(2), 107-19.

Valdez, L. A., Jaeger, E. C., Garcia, D. O., & Griffith, D. M. (2023, September–October). Breaking down machismo: Shifting definitions and embodiments of Latino manhood in middle-aged Latino men. *American Journal of Men's Health, 17*(5), 1-12.

Vande Kemp, H. (1996). Historical perspective: Religion and clinical psychology in America. In E. P. Shafranske (Ed.), *Religion and the clinical practice of psychology* (pp. 71-112). American Psychological Association.

Vazquez, V. E., & Knabb, J. J. (Eds.). (2023). Racial unity among Christian populations [Special issue]. *The Journal of Psychology & Christianity, 42*(2).

Vazquez, V., Knabb, J., Lee-Johnson, C., & Hays, K. (2023). *Healing conversations on race: Four key practices from Scripture and psychology*. IVP Academic.

Weisel-Barth, J. (2006). Thinking and writing about complexity theory in the clinical setting. *International Journal of Psychoanalytic Self Psychology, 1*(4), 365-88.

White, K. M. (2020). Conceptualizing therapy as a spiritual discipline. *Journal of Psychology and Christianity, 39*(2), 91-103.

Whitney, W. B., Dwiwardani, C., & Gonsalves, O. A. (2023). Why women's theological perspectives matter for teaching psychology. *Journal of Psychology and Christianity, 42*(1), 29-40.

Willard, D. (2002). *Renovation of the heart: Putting on the character of Christ*. NavPress.

Willard, D. (2006). *The great omission: Reclaiming Jesus's essential teachings on discipleship*. HarperSanFrancisco.

Williams, W. C. (1938). *The collected poems: volume 1, 1909–1939*. New Directions.

Witherington, B., III. (2004). *Paul's letter to the Romans: A socio-rhetorical commentary*. Eerdmans.

Wittgenstein, L. (2009). *Philosophical investigations* (4th ed.). Wiley-Blackwell.

Worthington, E. L., Johnson, E. L., Hook, J. N., & Aten, J. D. (Eds.). (2013). *Evidence-based practices for Christian counseling and psychotherapy*. IVP Academic.

Wright, R., Jones, P., & Strawn, B. D. (2014). Tradition-based integration. In *Christianity and psychoanalysis: A new conversation* (pp. 37-54). IVP Academic.

Yarhouse, M. A. (2019). *Sexual identity and faith: Helping clients find congruence*. Templeton.

Yarhouse, M. A., & Sadusky, J. A. (2022). *Gender identity and faith: Clinical postures, tools, and case studies for client-centered care*. IVP Academic.

Yun, D. (2003). *Sky, wind, and stars*. Translated by Kyung-Nyun Kim Richards and Steffen F. Richards. Asian Humanities Press.

Zahl, S. (2020). *The Holy Spirit and Christian experience*. Oxford University Press.

Zimmerman, J. (2012). *Incarnational humanism: A philosophy of culture of the church in the world*. IVP Academic.

Zuroski, E. (2020). *"Where do you know from?": An exercise in placing ourselves together in the classroom*. MAI. https://maifeminism.com/where-do-you-know-from-an-exercise-in-placing-ourselves-together-in-the-classroom/

NAME INDEX

Abu-Raiya, Hisham, 48
Adams, Jay E., 22
Allison, Elizabeth, 53, 147
Aten, Jamie D., 15
Atwood, George E., 65, 98, 125
Balswick, Jack O., 11
Barsness, Roy E., 93, 96-97, 99, 103, 151, 156
Beck, Richard, 139, 145
Békés, Vera, 158
Benjamin, Jessica A., 83, 86, 95
Benner, David G., 12, 131, 140, 145
Bland, Cayla S., 119
Bland, Earl D., 9, 12, 44, 71, 131, 137
Brenner, Charles, 95
Brown, Jeannine K., 19-20, 51
Brown, Warren S., 18-19, 44, 95, 130, 161
Browning, Don S., 73, 98
Buechler, Sandra, 148, 157, 165
Campbell, Clark D., 65
Carpenter, Angela, 12, 128-29
Carter, John D., 7, 10
Cates, Lorraine B., 121
Charles, Marilyn, 160
Coe, John H., 20, 131
Collicutt, Joanna, 12
Comas-Diaz, Lillian, 99
Cone, James H., 144
Cooper, Steven H., 157
Cooper, Terry D., 74, 98
Crisp, Thomas M., 12
Cushman, Philip, 37, 98, 101, 119
Doherty, William J., 103, 106
Dowling, Elizabeth M., 128
Du Bois, W. E. B., 72
Dueck, Alvin, 12, 18-19, 30, 67-68, 99, 100
Dwiwardani, Carissa, 137
Entwistle, David N., 10

Evans, C. Stephen, 160
Exline, Julie J., 16
Falzeder, Ernst, 155
Faw, Harold W., 10
Fisher, Lambers, 137
Flemming, Dean, 52
Fonagy, Peter, 53, 94, 147
Fors, Malin, 120
Fowler, James W., 128, 158
Freud, Sigmund, 96, 155, 162
Fromm, Erich, 100
Gadamer, Hans-Georg, 37, 44-45, 94
Garber, Steven, 162-63
Geertz, Clifford, 37, 150
Ghent, Emmanuel, 161
Greggo, Stephen P., 47-48, 51
Grenz, Stanley J., 128, 140
Griffin, Fred L., 160
Griffith, James L., 16
Griffith, Melissa Elliot, 16
Hall, M. Elizabeth Lewis, 13, 147
Hall, Todd W., 13, 20, 51, 131, 147
Halton, Charles, 144
Hamm, Dennis, 159
Hathaway, William L., 10, 14, 16, 37, 130
Haugen, Hans Morten, 128
Haynal, André, 155
Hays, Richard B., 142
Hazanov, Valery, 50
Hoard, Paul, 71
Hoffman, Marie T., 105, 155
James, William, 11-12
Jeeves, Malcolm A., 10, 13, 15, 91
Johnson, Eric L., 10, 13, 48, 52
Jones, Stanton L., 10, 56
Joshi, Khyati Y., 57
Knabb, Joshua, 11, 137

Lambert, Michael J., 151
Layton, Lynne, 41
Leclerc, Diane, 128
Ludwig, Thomas E., 10, 13, 15, 91
MacIntyre, Alasdair, 68, 69, 70, 72, 75, 99
Maddix, Mark A., 128
Malony, H. Newton, 10
McGuire, William, 155
McLaughlin, Paul T., 13
McMinn, Mark R., 13, 50, 65
McNeil, J. Derek, 57, 137
Milner, Marion, 118
Moon, Gary, 131-32
Murphy, Nancey, 52
Narramore, Bruce, 10
Neff, Megan Anne, 17, 50
Norcross, John C., 46, 151
Olthuis, James H., 131
Orange, Donna M., 61, 80
Pargament, Kenneth I., 16, 23, 87
Peterson, Eugene H., 145, 150
Polanyi, Michael, 46, 68, 126
Powlison, David, 22
Reed, Leah Fortson, 137
Reimer, Kevin, 12, 19, 30, 67-68, 100
Rennebohm, Samuel B., 152
Richardson, Frank C., 67, 98
Rivera, Edil Torres, 99
Sadusky, Julia A., 138
Sandage, Steven J., 15, 17, 19-20, 51, 137, 148
Sarnat, Joan E., 30
Scarlett, W. George, 128
Shults, F. LeRon, 148
Sisemore, Timothy A., 48, 51
Smith, James K. A., 72, 92
Smith, Linda B., 24, 118

Sorenson, Anita L., 51, 151
Sperry, Len, 16
Steere, David A., 131
Stern, Daniel N., 23
Stolorow, Robert D., 42, 65, 95, 98, 125
Strawn, Brad D., 8, 9, 12-15, 93, 95-97, 99, 103, 130-31, 137, 161
Suedfeld, Peter, 158
Sussman, Michael B., 123
Suttie, Ian D., 155
Tan, Shang-Yang, 21
Taylor, Charles, 37, 73, 94, 139-40
Thelen, Esther, 24, 118
Thoburn, John, 152
Tillich, Paul, 152
Tishby, Orya, 151
Tronick, Ed, 118, 121
Valdez, Luis A., 71
Vande Kemp, Hendrika, 8-10
Vazquez, Veola, 137
Weisel-Barth, Joye, 25
Wiseman, Hadas, 151
White, Kristen M., 131
Whitney, William B., 137
Willard, Dallas, 128, 154
Williams, William Carlos, 38, 40
Witherington, Ben, III, 130
Wittgenstein, Ludwig, 76, 82
Worthington, Everett L., 11, 141
Wright, Ron, 100
Yarhouse, Mark A., 10, 16, 130, 137
Yun Dong-ju, 39-40, 42
Zahl, Simeon, 128, 130, 141, 146
Zimmerman, Jens, 130, 133, 148
Zuroski, Eugenia, 116, 133

SUBJECT INDEX

acting out, 121
affectively salient, 146
apologetic wave, 9
applied/empirical validation wave, 9
biblical, 82-85, 87, 102, 141, 146
biblical counseling, 10, 22, 52
bracketing, 56, 67, 106, 119
Calvinism, 76-77
catastrophes, 24, 118
Catholicism, 72, 112-14, 116, 119, 124
class, 50, 82
    classism, 100
clinical integrative practice, 1-3, 15-16, 20-21, 31
clinical integrative wave, 9
code switching, 19
cognitive, 32, 60, 68
    behavioral, 65, 90, 97, 125
    pre-, 73
colonialism, 20, 98
complementarity, 82
complex dynamic system, 22-24, 28, 30, 167
complexity, 4, 10, 16, 19, 26-27, 30, 36, 61, 103, 115, 145, 150, 158, 161, 167
confusions of tongues, 76
countertransference enactments, 122
cultural linguistic model, 17-18
cultural liturgies, 72
cultural psychology, 69, 100
culture, 6, 7, 14, 18, 21-22, 30, 41-42, 46-47, 50, 55-56, 62-63, 68-70, 72, 76, 81, 86, 91-92, 94, 96, 98, 99-100, 103, 105, 107, 115-16, 127, 130, 137, 166
curiosity, 85, 138, 148, 161-62
dialogical, 3, 17-18, 101
disintegration, 31
dissociation, 121, 149, 154
distanciation, 59-60, 71, 103

diversity, 15, 137, 158, 160-61
double consciousness, 72
dynamic systems, 4, 23-24, 28, 31
embodied, 7, 12, 24, 26, 42, 50, 53, 95, 137, 142, 144-45, 150, 152, 161
emergent, 26, 28-29, 114, 128, 138, 144, 147
emergent model, 27
emergent property, 22, 57, 132
emergent process, 132
emerging integrative moments, 29, 49, 138
enactment, 30, 83-88, 122, 144
entangled, 22, 42, 44, 116-17, 130, 139-41, 148, 152
enlightenment, 69-70
epistemologies, 17
ethical critique of psychotherapy, 91
ethical reading, 80
ethics, 4, 8, 11, 27, 28-29, 56, 58, 62, 72-76, 84, 86-89, 92-109, 115, 120, 124, 126, 133, 157, 166
evangelicalism, 9, 14, 34, 55, 82, 124, 136
evidenced-based practices, 14
expectancy, 31, 138
experience near, 47, 142
explicit integration, 21-22
family resemblances, 76
family systems, 68, 125
five waves, 8
forgiveness, 14, 59
four strands of relational ethics, 92-106
gender, 21-22, 30, 36, 41-42, 50, 63, 71, 74, 79, 82-84, 86, 97, 100, 115, 117
good life, 4, 69, 70, 72-76, 79, 84, 86, 92, 98, 101, 106-7, 120
gratitude, 11, 14, 143
hermeneutics, 4, 8, 27-28, 37-38, 40-45, 49, 51-52, 56, 60-61, 77, 86, 88, 92, 97, 103, 105, 109, 133, 166

and circle, 43
and frame, 48, 62
and hospitality, 15
humility, 11, 14, 19, 31, 59, 104, 142, 161
immanence, 139-41, 144
implicit ethical systems, 99
implicit integration, 21
individualism, 70, 73, 99, 105, 107, 127
intersectional, 21, 30, 97, 116
intersubjective, 3, 51, 120, 131, 147
integrative mindset, 4, 45, 93
integrative moments, 4, 23, 25, 29-30, 31, 44-45, 49, 61, 109, 132, 138, 167
integrative thinking, 17
interpretation, 18, 20, 35, 37-41, 43, 60, 66, 84, 130, 158
invitation, 131-32, 154, 160, 164
Islam, 48, 111, 113-14, 124
kairos, 114
kenotic, 161
kingdom of God, 105, 123
lectio divina, 153-54
love, 6, 14, 39, 65, 74, 76, 91, 99, 104-5, 129, 131, 146-48, 150, 153-58, 161, 163, 165
mentalizing, 95
modeling wave, 9, 10, 13, 47
moral consultants, 103
moral discourse, 70, 93, 101, 106, 119
moral philosophies, 74, 98, 103
negative integration, 31, 57
normative unconscious, 41
objective truth, 53
observing ego, 95
openness, 23, 26, 129, 138
organizing principles, 50, 57, 65
personal-developmental integrative treatment plan, 166
personal ethical hermeneutic, 94
personhood, 21, 51
perspective taking, 59, 60
perturbations, 24
positive psychology, 14
practical moral cultures, 99
practical moral philosophies, 98, 103
practices, 9, 11-12, 14, 17-18, 21, 24, 26, 30, 55, 61, 68, 73-76, 79, 81-82, 84, 86-87, 102, 128-29, 131, 137-38, 140, 147, 151, 153-55, 157-58, 161-64, 166-67
    evidenced-based, 14
prejudice, 11, 49, 60, 94
preunderstandings, 94

propaedeutic, 45
psychoanalysis, 83, 97, 155
    psychoanalyst, 23, 61, 151, 156
    psychoanalytic, 23, 58, 80, 125, 151, 155
racism, 71, 74, 100
relational ethics, 92
relational model, 17, 19
relational schemas, 65
relational spirituality, 147, 151
resilience, 4, 8, 27-28, 62, 137-38, 147-49, 164, 166
resonance model of integration, 14
revelation, 138
self-development, 4, 8, 27-28, 166
self-organizing, 24, 27, 31
sexual orientation, 21-22, 30-31, 74, 79, 97
sin, 24, 31, 104, 123, 131, 145
social adjustment, 105
social imaginary, 73
social justice, 100
social location, 2-3, 14, 20, 28, 41, 52, 63, 66-67, 69, 71, 105-6, 116, 166
sovereignty of God, 27, 76-77, 87
spiritual development, 25, 128, 131
spiritual disciplines, 129, 131, 145
spiritual formation, 9, 12, 15, 16, 129-32
spiritual formation wave, 9
spiritual practices, 11, 128-29, 131, 140, 151, 154-55, 157, 161-64
spiritually integrated therapy, 16, 23, 87
splitting, 83, 121
supervision, 30, 34, 36, 46, 49-50, 65, 67, 78, 107, 110-12, 115, 135, 158
telos, 53, 92, 130, 147, 154
theory of mind, 94-95
thick faith, 150
third, the, 84-85
transcendence, 128, 138-139, 141-42
transference, 32-33, 122, 127, 144
    theological countertransference, 66
    transference-countertransference dynamics, 58, 83
tradition, 150, 153-55, 159-60, 166
tradition-based integration, 69
truth, 17-18, 20, 34, 41-43, 51-55, 59-61, 69, 85, 94-95, 99, 102, 120, 136, 147, 162
ultimate concerns, 73
uncertainty, 18, 32, 63, 149-51, 158, 162
unconscious organizing principles, 65
Wesleyanism, 17, 22, 47, 77, 104
white supremacy, 71

*An Association for Christian Psychologists,
Therapists, Counselors and Academicians*

CAPS is a vibrant Christian organization with a rich tradition. Founded in 1956 by a small group of Christian mental health professionals, chaplains and pastors, CAPS has grown to more than 2,100 members in the U.S., Canada and more than 25 other countries.

CAPS encourages in-depth consideration of therapeutic, research, theoretical and theological issues. The association is a forum for creative new ideas. In fact, their publications and conferences are the birthplace for many of the formative concepts in our field today.

CAPS members represent a variety of denominations, professional groups and theoretical orientations; yet all are united in their commitment to Christ and to professional excellence.

CAPS is a non-profit, member-supported organization. It is led by a fully functioning board of directors, and the membership has a voice in the direction of CAPS.

CAPS is more than a professional association. It is a fellowship, and in addition to national and international activities, the organization strongly encourages regional, local and area activities which provide networking and fellowship opportunities as well as professional enrichment.

To learn more about CAPS, visit www.caps.net.

The joint publishing venture between IVP Academic and CAPS aims to promote the understanding of the relationship between Christianity and the behavioral sciences at both the clinical/counseling and the theoretical/research levels. These books will be of particular value for students and practitioners, teachers and researchers.

For more information about CAPS Books, visit InterVarsity Press's website at www.ivpress.com/christian-association-for-psychological-studies-books-set.